Liverpool Everyman & Playhouse present the world première of

# HOPE PLACE

By Michael Wynne

**First performed on 9 May 2014 at the Everyman theatre Liverpool**

# LIVERPOOL EVERYMAN & PLAYHOUSE

## Two Great Theatres.
## One Creative Heart.

**We are two distinct theatres, almost a mile apart, which together make up a single artistic force.**

For over 10 years we have been driven by our passion for our art-form, our love of our city and our unswerving belief that theatre at its best can enhance lives. While our two performances bases could hardly be more different, they are united by our commitment to brilliant, humane, forward-thinking theatre that responds to its time and place.

At the beating heart of the theatres is our work with writers; since it is our passionate belief that an investment in new writing is an investment in our theatrical future. Our mission is to nurture and develop the playwrights who will represent the city's talent, its voice and its unique energy, whilst at the same time showcasing new work by established local, national and international playwrights. In the last ten years we have produced 38 world premières across the two theatres, three quarters of which were by Liverpool writers. Of these, 10 were debut plays and 15 of the productions toured or transferred.

It's an exciting time for new writing at the Everyman & Playhouse. Our wide-ranging support for writers includes an annual Young Writers' Programme; a Writers On Attachment scheme; and the annual festival of new work and ideas, *Everyword*. And most wonderfully, the new Everyman has a Writers' Room where writers can work, research and meet to ferment ideas.

---

For more information about the Everyman & Playhouse, including the full programme and activities such as playwright support visit:

### www.everymanplayhouse.com or call 0151 709 4776

Twitter.com/LivEveryPlay
Flickr.com/LivEveryPlay
Instagram.com/LivEveryPlay

Facebook.com/everymanplayhouse
Youtube.com/everymanplayhouse

---

**Sign up to receive our e-newsletter via our website, and we'll keep you posted on what's coming up, casting information, previews and reviews.**

Liverpool Everyman & Playhouse are a registered charity (1081229) and gratefully acknowledge the support of our funders, donors and audiences.

**For their ongoing financial support, we would like to thank:**

ESMÉE FAIRBAIRN FOUNDATION, THE LEVERHULME TRUST
PAUL HAMLYN FOUNDATION, KNOWSLEY MBC

**Our Principal Partner:**

Liverpool John Moores University

**Our Business Members and Sponsors:**

Benson Signs, Bolland & Lowe, Bruntwood, Cobhams Tax Consultants & Accountants,
Duncan Sheard Glass, EEF, Exterion Media, Hope Street Hotel, Liverpool City Region LEP,
Mando, Merseytravel, NW Systems Group, Synergy, Wrightsure Insurance Group

**Those who have left us a legacy:**

Dorothy Smellie
Anni Parker & Brian Barry
Malcolm and Roger Frood in memory of Graham and Joan Frood

And all the individual donors listed on our website at
**www.everymanplayhouse.com**

# Credits

## Cast (in alphabetical order)

| | |
|---|---|
| **Michelle Butterly** | Barb, Sarah, Lottie Byrne, Minkie, Monica, Carla, Lily Lloyd |
| **Neil Caple** | Eric |
| **Ciaran Kellgren** | Simon |
| **Tricia Kelly** | Veronica |
| **Emma Lisi** | Josie |
| **Joe McGann** | Jack |
| **Eileen O'Brien** | Maggie |
| **Alan Stocks** | Farmer, Richard Byrne, Mr Maguire, Craig, Jonathan, Rob, Roger |
| | |
| **Freya Barnes** | Young Veronica |
| **Julia Carlile** | Young Veronica |
| **Kaitlyn Hogg** | Young Maggie, Girl |
| **Rumah Norton** | Young Maggie, Girl |
| **Frank Turpin** | Young Eric |
| **George Turpin** | Young Eric |
| **Harry Turpin** | Young Jack, Cinema Kid |
| **Sam Vaughan** | Young Jack, Cinema Kid |

## Special thanks
Sylvie Gatrill from Allstars Casting **www.allstarscasting.co.uk**
The Royal Court (London) and Davinia Hamilton-Maddox

## Company

| | |
|---|---|
| Writer | **Michael Wynne** |
| Director | **Rachel Kavanaugh** |
| Designer | **Peter McKintosh** |
| Lighting Designer | **Tim Lutkin** |
| Sound Designer | **Fergus O'Hare** |
| Composer | **Isobel Waller-Bridge** |
| Casting Director | **Kay Magson CDG** |
| Costume Supervisor | **Jacquie Davies** |
| | |
| Production Manager | **Sean Pritchard** |
| Company Manager | **Sarah Lewis** |
| Stage Manager | **Xenia Lewis** |
| Deputy Stage Manager | **Roxanne Vella** |
| Assistant Stage Manager | **Gemma Dunne** |
| Lighting Programmer | **Lorraine Marshall** |
| LX & AV Technicians | **Xenia Bayer & Rob Newman** |
| Wardrobe Maintenance | **Tracey Thompson** |
| Dresser | **Jess Schofield** |
| Set Construction | **Splinter** |
| Scenic Print | **Gary Chase at Service Graphics** |

## MICHELLE BUTTERLY
Barb, Sarah, Lottie Byrne,
Minkie, Monica, Carla,
Lily Lloyd

**Theatre credits include:** *Blair's Children* (Cockpit Theatre); *Queen of the Nile* (Hull Truck Theatre); *Dead Heavy Fantastic* (Liverpool Everyman); *Noughts and Crosses* (Royal Shakespeare Company and tour); *Ma Vie En Rose* (Young Vic); *I Like Mine With a Kiss* (Bush Theatre); *Speaking Like Magpies, A New Way To Please You, Believe What You Will* and *Thomas More* (Royal Shakespeare Company/Stratford and Trafalgar Studios); *Gone to Earth* (Shared Experience / Tour); *The People Are Friendly* (Royal Court); *A Servant to Two Masters* (Royal Shakespeare Company and West End); *Road* and *Shakers* (Wolsey Theatre, Ipswich); *End of the Food Chain* (Stephen Joseph Theatre); *Laundry Room at the Hotel Madrid* (Gate Theatre, London); *Lent* (Belgrade Studio, Coventry) and *Gaslight* (Theatr Clwyd).

**Television credits include:** *Benidorm* (Series Regular); *Beautiful People* (Series 1 and 2), *Midsomer Murders, Doctors, Minder, No Angels* (Series 2); *Eyes Down, Dangerfield, Pie in the Sky, Hetty Wainthrop Investigates, Soldier Soldier, St Clare, The Echo, Heartbeat* and *Casualty.*

## NEIL CAPLE
Eric

**Theatre credits include:** *Accidental Death of an Anarchist* (Northern Broadsides and Tour*); Twelfth Night, Macbeth* and *Billy Wonderful* (Liverpool Everyman) *Unprotected* (Liverpool Everyman and Traverse, Edinburgh); *The Misanthrope* and *The Hypochondriac* (Liverpool Playhouse and ETT Tour); *The Servant of Two Masters, The Warehouse, The Flint Street Nativity, Breezeblock Park* and *The Odd Couple* (Liverpool Playhouse); *Funny Money, Lost Soul, On the Ledge* and *Two* (Royal Court, Liverpool); *Othello* (Watermill Theatre Company and Tokyo); *The Merry Wives of Windsor, The Wind In The Willows, The Trackers of Oxyrynchus* and *Strangeways* (Royal National Theatre); *A Comedy of Errors* and *Macbeth* (Royal Shakespeare Company); *The Front Page* (Donmar Warehouse); *Much Ado About Nothing* and *Julius Caesar* (Regents Park) and *Waterland* (Shaw).

**Television credits include:** *Justice, Far from the Madding Crowd, Cadfael, The Bullion Boys, Civvies, Casualty, Holby City, The Bill, Coronation St, Brookside, Doctors, Pygmalion* and *Lee & Herring's Fist of Fun.*

**Radio credits include:** Neil has appeared in over 20 plays for Radio 4, read the *Morning Story* and been a regular on *Weekending.*

**Film credits include:** *Best, Out of Depth, Rebecca's Daughters* and *No Way Out!*

## CIARAN KELLGREN
Simon

**Theatre credits include:** *No More Page 3* (Park Theatre); *Wanted: Robin Hood* and *The Heretic* (Library Theatre Company); *Golden Dragon* (India, Iraq, Ireland tours); *Poppy, Fashion* (RSC), *TERROR* (Soho Theatre); *Peter Pan* (Kensington Gardens, o2 Arena); *Eric's* and *Macbeth* (Liverpool Everyman); *Twopence to cross the Mersey* (Liverpool Empire) and *Christmas Carol* (Liverpool Playhouse).

**Film credits include:** *Goodbye heart, Tom and Lilli* and *Beyond Time*.

**Television credits include:** *Sex and the Chippy, Casualty, Shameless, The Unsinkable Titanic, Doctors* and *Cold Blood*.

## TRICIA KELLY
Veronica

Tricia's first job in theatre was as Assistant Stage Manager for the 1974/5 Everyman season. She returned to appear in *Unprotected* which won an Amnesty Human Rights award when it played the Traverse in Edinburgh.

**Other theatre credits include:** *Man To Man* (Mercury Theatre Colchester); *Responsible Other* (Made by Brick/Hampstead Downstairs); *Cannibals* and *The Gatekeeper* –Best Studio Performance nomination Manchester Theatre Awards (Royal Exchange, Manchester); *The Kitchen* (National Theatre); *Uncle Vanya* (Arcola Theatre/Belgrade); *Tiger Country* and *The Maths Tutor* (Hampstead Theatre); *Pieces Of Vincent* (Arcola); *This Wide Night* (Bernie Grant); *Blue Heaven* (Finborough); *When We Are Married* (West Yorkshire /Liverpool Playhouse); *The Life & Adventures Of Nicholas Nickleby* (West End/Chichester/UK tour/Toronto); *Unprotected* (Liverpool Everyman/Traverse); *Some Explicit Polaroids* (Out Of Joint - UK & US tour); *Ion* and *Julius Caesar* (Royal Shakespeare Company); *Inland Sea* (Oxford Stage/Wilton's Music Hall); *Local* (Royal Court Theatre Upstairs); *A Wife Without A Smile, The House Among The Stars, The Cassilis Engagement, The Way Of The World* and *The Choice* (Orange Tree); *The Seagull, The Government Inspector* and *As You Like It* (Sheffield Crucible); *Barbarians, Dancing At Lughnasa* and *Jamaica Inn* (Salisbury); *Season's Greetings, A Whisper Of Angel's Wings* and *Julius Caesar* (Birmingham Rep); *King Lear, Not I, Two* and *Sunsets & Glories* (West Yorkshire Playhouse); *The Voysey Inheritance (*Edinburgh Lyceum); *Amphytryo*n (The Gate); *Venus & Lucrece* (Almeida); *Victory* (Wrestling School/Greenwich); *Seven Lears, Golgo, Et In Arcadia Ego* and *The Last Supper* (Wrestling School/Royal Court Theatre); *Fen* (also New York), *A Mouthful Of Birds* and *Deadlines* (Joint Stock/Royal Court); *Top Girls* (Lancaster);*The Country Wife* and *Just Between Ourselves* (Belgrade) and *Saturday Night & Sunday Morning* (Nottingham Playhouse).

**Television and film credits include:** *Eastenders, My Family, Casualty, The Bill, High Stakes, In Sickness and in Health, It's History, Gran, Christobel, Dangerous Lady, A Small Dance, Top Dog* and *Real Lies*.

**Radio credits include:** *Pilgrim, St Brice's Day, A Year and a Day* and *Kes*.

## EMMA LISI
Josie

**Theatre credits include:** *Liverbirds.com, Talking Heads* and *Two* (Liverpool Actors Studio); *Blood Brothers* (Theatre Royal, St Helens) and *Les Liaisons Dangereuses, The Wild Party, Book Ends, Burnt by the Sun, The Madras House, The Recruiting Officer, A Doll's House* and *Henry IV Part 1* (Bristol Old Vic Theatre School).

**Film credits include:** *The Crew.*

## JOE MCGANN
Jack

**Theatre credits include:** *Love Billy* (Lyric, Belfast); *The Rise And Fall Of Little Voice* (National Tour); *The Resistible Rise Of Arturo Ui* (Chichester Theatre and Duchess Theatre, West End); *Calendar Girls 3* (National Tours David Pugh Ltd); *No Expense Spared* (Jermyn Street Theatre); *Lost Monsters* (Liverpool Everyman); *Fiddler On The Roof* (National Tour); *Guys And Dolls* (ATG UK Tour); *Tom, Dick And Harry* (Duke of York's Theatre); *An Immaculate Misconception* (Singapore Repertory Theatre); *Of Mice And Men* (Old Vic); *Take A Chance On Me* (New End, Hampstead); *Wonderful Tennessee* (Nottingham Playhouse); *Earth And Sky* (National Tour); *Live Bed Show* (National Tour); *Silhouette* (National Tour); *Cat On A Hot Tin Roof* (National Tour); *Oliver* (Palladium); *One Fine Day* (Liverpool Playhouse & Albery Theatre); *Of Mice And Men* (Nottingham Playhouse); *Crooked Wood* (King's Head); *The Long & The Short & The Tall* (National Tour); *Guys And Dolls* (Haymarket Theatre, Leicester); *The Resistible Rise Of Arturo Ui* and *Canterbury Tales* (Crucible Theatre, Sheffield); *Jack And The Beanstalk In The Wild, Wild West* (Young Vic); *Blood Brothers* (National Tour); *Yakety Yak* (Half Moon Theatre Co & Astoria) and *The Water Babies* and *The Gondoliers* (Chichester Festival Theatre).

**Television credits include:** *Casualty, My Family, Casualty 24, I Shouldn't Be Alive, Celebrity Masterchef, Liverpool Nativity, Mersey Beat, Doctors, Night And Day, Heartbeat, Madame Bovary, Dangerfield, The Hanging Gale, The Upper Hand, The Harry Enfield Show, All Creatures Great And Small, The Chronicles Of Narnia, Prince Caspian: Part 2, Norbert Smith, Rockliffe's Babies, The Brothers McGregor, The Gentle Touch* and *Johnny Jarvis.*

**Film credits include:** *Limescale, Splinter, Puckoon, Brylcream Boys, No Surrender* and *Food Of Love*

## EILEEN O'BRIEN
Maggie

**Theatre credits include:** *Forget-Me-Not* (Belvoir Theatre, Sydney); *What You Will* (Shakespeare's Globe – Pop Up); *Macbeth* (Liverpool Everyman); *'Tis Pity She's A Whore* and *Anthology* (Everyman Unbound Season: Liverpool Everyman/Slung Low) (Best Actress Award – Liverpool Daily Post Arts Awards); *When We Are Married* (West Yorkshire Playhouse/Liverpool Playhouse); *Death of a Salesman* (York Theatre Royal); *The Revenger's Tragedy, Basil and Beattie, Across Oka, Rafts and Dreams, Yerma, Prize Night; The Plough and the Stars* (Royal Exchange Theatre, Manchester); *An Inspector Calls* (Oldham Coliseum); *The Crucible* and *The Beauty Queen of Leenane* (Bolton Octagon); *Kindertransport* (Best Actress Award – Liverpool Daily Post Arts Awards) and *A Doll's House* (Shared Experience); *Foxes* (West Yorkshire Playhouse); *On the Shore of the Wild World* (National Theatre/Royal Exchange Theatre, Manchester); *Beyond Belief* and *Death of a Salesman* (Manchester Library); *Redundant* and *The Knocky* (the Royal Court Theatre) and *Richard III* and *We Are Three Sisters* (Northern Broadsides).

**Television credits include:** *Being Eileen, Holby City, Lennon Naked, Moving On, Red in Tooth and Claw, Doctors, The Royal Today, Emmerdale, Casualty, Eyes Down, Building the Titanic, The Royal, Merseybeat, The Vice, Brookside, The Life and Crimes of William Palmer, The Practise* and *Boys from the Blackstuff*.

**Film credits include:** *Before Dawn, Fanny and Elvis, A Private Function, A Month in the Country* and *Runners*.

**Radio credits include:** *The Diddakoi, The Judas Burner, ID, Legacy, Calagari, Tin Man* and *Snow in July*.

## ALAN STOCKS
Farmer, Richard Byrne, Mr Maguire, Craig, Jonathan, Rob, Roger

Alan trained at RADA.

**Theatre credits include:** *Held, A Streetcar Named Desire, Tartuffe* and *Flint Street Nativity* (Liverpool Playhouse); *Twelfth Night, Sleeping Beauty, Love at a Loss, 'Tis Pity She's A Whore, Wild Wild Women, Trojan Women* and *Dead Heavy Fantastic* (Liverpool Everyman); *Measure for Measure, The Two Gentlemen of Verona* and *the Merchant of Venice* (Royal Shakespeare Company); *Twelfth Night* (Lyric Belfast); *End of the Food Chain* (Stephen Joseph Theatre) and *Nervous Breakdown* (Warehouse Theatre). He recently toured *Tartuffe* on an ETT national tour.

**Television credits include:** *Phone Shop, Casualty 1907, Kingdom, Robin Hood, Ghost Boat, Blue Blood, Wire in the Blood, The Plan man, Rome, Merseybeat, This Little Life, Auf Wiedersehen Pet, City Central, Dad, Drop the Dead Donkey, Murder in Mind, North Square, Sins, Dockers, This Life, Wycliffe, Grushko, The Day Today, Soldier Soldier, Conviction, Between the Lines, Sweet Nothing* and *You Me And Him* amongst others.

**Film credits include:** *Memory of Water, The Birthday Girl, Under Suspicion, Trigger Puller, The Pond* and *Look At Me I'm Beautiful*.

**Radio credits include:** *Tartuffe*.

## MICHAEL WYNNE
### Writer

Michael Wynne is an Olivier Award winning playwright. His first play, *The Knocky*, was performed at the Royal Court Theatre and Liverpool Everyman · and was awarded the Meyer Whitworth Award for Best New Play and Liverpool Echo Arts Award for Best New Talent.

**Other plays include:** *The People Are Friendly* and *The Priory* (Royal Court), which won the Laurence Olivier Award for Best Comedy; *Dirty Wonderland* and *Sell Out* (Frantic Assembly), which won Time Out Best Off West End Play Award; *The Boy Who Left Home* (Actors Touring Company/ Lyric Hammersmith); *Tits/Teeth* (Soho Theatre/NYT) and *Canvas* (Chichester).

**He also writes for TV and film, including:** *Being Eileen* and *Lapland* (BBC1) and he co-wrote *My Summer of Love* (BBC Films), which won the BAFTA for Best British Film and, Evening Standard Film Awards for Best Screenplay.

**Other Television credits include:** *Substance, Eyes Down, UGetMe* and *Mayo* (BBC); *Little Crackers/Sheridan Smith/The Daltons* (Sky1); *Grafters, Where The Heart Is* and *Don't Eat the Neighbours* (ITV) and *As If* and *Sugar Rush* (Channel 4).

## RACHEL KAVANAUGH
### Director

Rachel's most recent production, the hugely successful *The Sound of Music*, at Regent's Park Open Air Theatre, has been nominated for an Olivier Award. Later this year she will be directing *An Ideal Husband* for the Chichester Festival Theatre.

**Other productions directed at Chichester include:** *The Way of the World, The Music Man* and *A Small Family Business*. Her last West End production, *Love Story*, transferred from Chichester to the Duchess Theatre and subsequently to the Walnut Street Theatre, Philadelphia.

As Artistic Director of the Birmingham Rep for five years, Rachel directed *Arthur and George, His Dark Materials, Hapgood, Peter Pan – a Musical Adventure, Uncle Vanya, The Wizard of Oz, Racing Demon, Murmuring Judges, The Madness of George III, A Doll's House (*also toured), and *Arcadia* (with Bristol Old Vic).

**For the Royal Shakespeare Company:** *Alice in Wonderland* and *The Merry Wives of Windsor.*

**For the Regents Park Open Air Theatre:** *The Taming of the Shrew, As You Like It, Love's Labours' Lost, Twelfth Night, A Midsummer Night's Dream, Cymbeline, Much Ado About Nothing, Twelfth Night* and *Two Gentlemen of Verona.*

**Other theatre credits include:** *Guys and Dolls* (Sheffield Crucible); *Hilda* (Hampstead); *A View from the Bridge* (Greenwich); *Eva Peron, The Walls* and *Saigon Rose* (Orange Tree Theatre).

## PETER MCKINTOSH
Designer

Peter won the 2012 Olivier Award for 'Best Costume Design' for *Crazy For You* at Regent's Park Open Air Theatre and in the West End. His designs for *The 39 Steps* (London, Broadway and Worldwide) were nominated for 'Best Scenic Design of a Play' and 'Best Costume Design of a Play' at the 2008 Tony Awards.

**His other theatre credits include:**
*The Winslow Boy* (Old Vic/Broadway); *Noises Off* (Old Vic/West End); *The Sound of Music* (Regent's Park); *Dirty Rotten Scoundrels, Another Country, Relatively Speaking, Viva Forever, Death and The Maiden, Butley, Love Story, Prick Up Your Ears, Entertaining Mr. Sloane, Donkey's Years, The Dumb Waiter, Fiddler On The Roof, A Woman of No Importance, Boston Marriage, Educating Rita* and *Shirley Valentine* (West End); *The Doctor's Dilemma, Honk!* and *Widower's House* (The National Theatre); *King John, Brand Pericles, Alice In Wonderland* and *The Merry Wives of Windsor* (Royal Shakespeare Company); *Luise Miller, Serenading Louie, The Chalk Garden, Be Near Me, The Cryptogram* and ***John Gabriel Borkman*** (Donmar Warehouse); *The Turn of the Screw, The Knot of the Heart, Waste, Cloud Nine* and *Romance* (Almeida) and *The Heretic* (Royal Court).

**Opera credits include world premieres of:** *The Handmaid's Tale* at Royal Danish Opera & English National Opera, *The Marriage of Figaro* for English National Opera, and the UK premiere of Michael Nyman's *Love Counts* for Almeida Opera.

## TIM LUTKIN
Lighting Designer

Tim is a graduate of the Guildhall School of Music & Drama.

**Theatre credits include:** *Strangers On A Train* (Gielgud); *Chimerica* (Almeida/Pinter); *Candide* and *All's Well That Ends Well* (Royal Shakespeare Company); *Minotaur* (Polka Theatre); *Once A Catholic* (Tricycle & Royal Court Liverpool); *The Full Monty* (Noel Coward and UK Tour); *Calendar Girls* (UK Tours); *Ghost - The Musical* (UK Tour - co-design with Hugh Vanstone); *Philadelphia Here I Come!* (Donmar); *Megan Mullally & Supreme Music Program* and *Alan Cumming - I Bought a Blue Car Today* (Vaudeville); *Party* (Arts); *The Dark At The Top Of The Stairs* (Belgrade, Coventry); *Our Brother David* (Watford Palace); *Wondershow* (Roundhouse); *The Go Between* (West Yorkshire Playhouse); *Bronte* (Shared Experience); *The Rime of the Ancient Mariner* (Royal Festival Hall); *My Dad's a Birdman* (Crucible, Sheffield); *That Face* (Tron, Glasgow); *Restoration* (Salisbury Playhouse); *Fuchsia* (White Bear); *Lucky You* (Assembly Rooms) and *The Calling of Maisy Day* (Welsh National Opera).

## FERGUS O'HARE
Sound Designer

**Liverpool Everyman & Playhouse credits include:** *Twelfth Night, The Misanthrope, A Streetcar Named Desire, Macbeth, No Wise Men, Tartuffe, Our Country's Good, The Electric Hills, Intemperance* and *Guiding Star.*

**Other theatre credits include:** *The Things We Do For Love* (Theatre Royal Bath); *Relative Values* (Pinter Theatre); *Another Country* (Tafalgar Studios); *Pygmalion* (Cambridge Arts/Tour); *King Lear* (Chichester/BAM); *The Jungle Book* (West Yorkshire Playhouse); *In the Next Room or The Vibrator Play* (St. James Theatre); *Passion Play* (Duke of York's); *The Winslow Boy* (Old Vic/Roundabout); *Street Scene* (Theatre du Chatelet, Paris/ Gran Teatro del Liceu, Barcelona); *Macbeth* (NTS/ Barrymore. Drama Desk nominee. Broadway World Award); *No Quarter* (Royal Court); *The Arthur Conan Doyle Appreciation Society* (Traverse); *Glasgow Girls* (National Theatre of Scotland/Citz/Theatre Royal Stratford East); *Romeo and Juliet* (Corcadorca at Cork Opera House); *A Chorus of Disapproval* (Pinter Theatre); *Opening Ceremony of the 2012 London Paralympic Games* (Olympic Park, Stratford).

## ISOBEL WALLER-BRIDGE
Composer

Isobel trained at Edinburgh University, Kings College London and the Royal Academy of Music.

**Theatre credits as Composer and Sound Designer include:** *Yellow Face* (National Theatre); *Fleabag* (Soho); *Not The Worst Place* (Paines Plough); *Incognito* (Live Theatre/ High Tide/Bush); *Orlando* (Royal Exchange Manchester); *King Lear* (Chichester/BAM); *Neville's Island* and *If Only* (Chichester Festival Theatre); *Forever House* (Theatre Royal Plymouth); *Sleuth* (Watermill Theatre); *Gruesome Playground Injuries* (Gate Theatre); *Mydidae* (Soho Theatre and Trafalgar Studios); *Blink* (Traverse Theatre and Soho Theatre); *The Girl with the Iron Claws* (Arcola Theatre).

**Credits as Musical Director include:** *A Woman Killed with Kindness* (National Theatre) and *A Christmas Carol* (Library Theatre Manchester). Credits as Music

**Associate and Musician include:** *The Children's Hour* (Comedy Theatre) and *Rocket to the Moon* and *Welcome to Thebes* (National Theatre).

**Television, film and radio credits as Composer include:** *The Frozen Planet: The Making Of* (BBC), *Freeze Frames, Secret Symphony* (Samsung/Times), *Gilead, Physics, Ellie, Disaffected, Beautiful Enough, Hometown* and *Meeting Mr Tiller.* Credits as Orchestrator/Arranger include: *The Imposter, Life, Planet Earth Live!, The Bounty Hunter, The Day of the Flowers* and *Route Irish.*

## KAY MAGSON CDG
Casting Director

**Theatre credits include:** *Macbeth*, *Dead Heavy Fantastic* (Liverpool Everyman); *'Tis Pity She's a Whore* and *Anthology* (Liverpool Everyman/Slung Low); *Aladdin, Jack and the Beanstalk* and *Cinderella* (Liverpool Playhouse); *Kes* (Liverpool Playhouse and national tour); *The Solid Gold Cadillac* (Garrick); *Dangerous Corner* (West Yorkshire Playhouse/West End); *Round the Horne...Revisited* and *Dracula* (national tours); *Singin' in the Rain* (West Yorkshire Playhouse/National Theatre and national tour); *Aspects of Love*, *All the Fun of the Fair* and *The Witches of Eastwick* (national tours); *Great Expectations* (ETT/Watford/national tour) and *Sweeney Todd* (Royal Festival Hall), *Crime and Punishment* (Glasgow Citz/Liverpool Playhouse), *Kes* and *Cooking with Elvis* (Derby Theatre) and *Sherlock* (West Yorkshire Playhouse & national tour).

Kay was resident at the West Yorkshire Playhouse for 17 years where she cast many shows including: *Hamlet*, the McKellen ensemble season, the Patrick Stewart Priestley season and many others, and also casts regularly for Perth, West Yorkshire Playhouse, Hull Truck, Derby Theatre, Glasgow Citz, English Theatre Frankfurt and the Manchester Library Theatre.

Kay is a member of the Casting Directors Guild of Great Britain (CDG).

## JACQUIE DAVIES
Costume Supervisor

**Theatre credits include:** *A View from the Bridge*, *Aladdin*, *A Day in the Death of Joe Egg*, *The Misanthrope*, *Jack and the Beanstalk*, *The Alchemist*, *The Norman Conquests*, *A Streetcar Named Desire*, *Cinderella*, *The Resistible Rise of Arturo Ui*; *Oedipus*, *Canary*, *Ghost Stories*, *The Hypochondriac*, *The Price*, *Our Country's Good*, *Tartuffe* and *Once Upon a Time at the Adelphi* (Liverpool Playhouse); *Scrappers*, *Held*, *The Match Box* (Liverpool Playhouse Studio); *Twelfth Night*, *Macbeth*, *Dead Heavy Fantastic*, *Sleeping Beauty*, *'Tis Pity She's a Whore*, *Anthology*, *The Ragged Trousered Philanthropists*, *Dick Whittington*, *The Caretaker*, *Lost Monsters*, *Billy Wonderful*, *Mother Goose*, *Endgame*, *Eric's*, *Intemperance*, *The Way Home*, *The Morris* and *Port Authority* (Liverpool Everyman); *Vurt*, *Wise Guys*, *Unsuitable Girls* and *Perfect* (Contact Theatre, Manchester); *Oleanna* and *Memory* (Clwyd Theatr Cymru); *Love on the Dole* (the Lowry, Manchester); *Never the Sinner* (Library Theatre, Manchester) and *Shockheaded Peter* (West End).

**Opera credits include work at:** Scottish Opera, Buxton Opera Festival, Music Theatre Wales and Opera Holland Park.

**Television and film credits include:** *Queer As Folk*, *The Parole Officer*, *I Love the 1970s* and *1980s*, *Brookside* and *Hollyoaks*.

**Design credits include:** *Kes*, *Saturday, Sunday, Monday*, *Oh What a Lovely War*, *Into the Woods*, *The Rover*, *Titus Andronicus*, *Pericles*, *Spring Awakening*, *Twelfth Night*, *Macbeth*, *The Red Balloon*, *The Weirdstone of Brisingamen*, *Perfect*, *The Cherry Orchard*, *Machinal* and *Trelawny of the 'Wells'*.

## Hope Place

Michael Wynne was born and brought up in Birkenhead.
His first play, *The Knocky*, was performed at the Royal
Court Theatre: it was awarded the Meyer Whitworth
Award for Best New Play, and he was nominated for
Best New Writer by the Writers Guild. Other plays
include *The People Are Friendly* (Royal Court), nominated
for Best Comedy, WhatsOnStage Awards; *The Priory*
(Royal Court), which won the Laurence Olivier Award
for Best Comedy and was nominated for Best Comedy,
WhatsOnStage Awards; *Sell Out* (Frantic Assembly),
which won *Time Out* Best Off West End Award; *The
Boy Who Left Home* (Actor Touring Company); *Dirty
Wonderland* (Frantic Assembly); *Tits / Teeth* (Soho Theatre/
NYT); and *Canvas* (Minerva Theatre, Chichester). He
also writes for TV and film, including *Lapland* and *Being
Eileen* (both BBC1), and co-wrote *My Summer of Love*
(BBC Films), which won the BAFTA for Best British Film
and *Evening Standard* Film Award for Best Screenplay.

*also by Michael Wynne from Faber*

THE KNOCKY
THE PRIORY
THE PEOPLE ARE FRIENDLY
CANVAS

# MICHAEL WYNNE

# Hope Place

FABER & FABER

First published in 2014
by Faber and Faber Limited
74–77 Great Russell Street, London WC1B 3DA

Typeset by Country Setting, Kingsdown, Kent CT14 8ES
Printed in England by CPI Group (UK) Ltd, Croydon CR0 4YY

A CIP record for this book is available from the British Library

ISBN 978–0–571–31816–2

FSC
www.fsc.org
MIX
Paper from
responsible sources
FSC® C101712

2 4 6 8 10 9 7 5 3 1

For my mother
Johanna Wynne

## Acknowledgements

A huge thank you to:
Lindsay Rodden, Gemma Bodinetz,
Michael McCoy, Rachel Kavanaugh,
Frank Gilmore, Sheila Gilmore,
Pauline Gilmore, Johanna Wynne,
Helen Robinson, Rachel Millard,
Paul Keating, Debra Oswald,
Rib Davis, Christine Gibbons,
Brene Brown and all the Lowrys

# Characters

Farmer
Girl
Jack
Eric
Veronica
Maggie
Barb
Josie
Simon
Young Maggie
Mr Maguire
Sarah
Young Jack
Young Eric
Lottie
Young Veronica
Richard
Craig
Minkie
Kitty
Jonathan
Monica
Rob
Carla
Lily
Roger

# HOPE PLACE

If you cannot get rid of the family skeleton,
you may as well make it dance.

*George Bernard Shaw*

# Prologue

*Caption – all captions are to be seen by the audience:*

## HERE

### 1699

*High up on a large misty ridge that was to become Hope Street, Liverpool. We're surrounded by wide open fields and muddy bogs. A couple of windmills in the distance. The sound of seagulls. It's a blustery day, the wind whipping by.*

*A young girl, aged eight, appears out of the mist. She looks out with a sense of wonder, taking the view in. She walks forward and stumbles. A farmer appears behind her.*

**Farmer** Watch the bog my girl. Fall into that and you'll never be seen again.

*He takes her hand and leads her across the bog.*

That's better. It eats people up this bog.

**Girl** Really?

**Farmer** Oh yes. You'll be walking along and see a foot sticking out or the top of someone's hat. The ones that weren't so lucky.

*They stop and look out.*

Now, look at all that down there. I said I'd bring you up here one day and show you it all. Isn't it wonderful?

**Farmer** Fields and fields and fields. Look. Can you see the castle?

**Girl** Yes, yes.

**Farmer** That's where King John lived. And he had a huge dragon. A monster of a beast. Breathed fire and ate children. Would have eaten you right up in one mouthful.

**Girl** Is that true?

**Farmer** Of course.

**Farmer** The King turned this from a little fishing village into what it is now. They say there's about five hundred people living here now.

**Girl** That many?

**Farmer** This is just the beginning. One day there'll be maybe . . . six hundred people here. See the river? And the ships?

*She nods.*

There'll be more and more ships coming here. I'm telling you. Get on one of those ships and who knows where you'll end up.

**Girl** I love it up here.

**Farmer** Some call it 'Elverpool' because they say the pool, the river, is full of eels. There's some parts of the river that are so full of eels there's no water. All wriggling about. If you fall in they eat you. (*Beat.*) Just like that dragon. (*Beat.*) And the bog.

**Girl** I don't like that.

**Farmer** Don't be frightened.

**Girl** I never know if you're telling me the truth or a story.

**Farmer** My father used to bring me up here and tell me stories. You'll do the same with your children. We pass the stories on.

*He looks out.*

I love a good story.

*The wind whips up and the scene changes.*

# Act One

## SCENE ONE

*8 Hope Place. Basement kitchen. Modern day.*
*A classic-looking kitchen, quite minimal – it could*
*be from any period. Back door to the yard on one side,*
*door to the rest of the house on the other side. An open*
*doorway into a larder behind. Large table in the middle*
*covered in trays of food – sandwiches, sausage rolls,*
*cake. Cooker and sink behind. A winding staircase on the*
*right leads up to the rest of the house. Jack and Eric sit*
*at the table, drinking. Their sister, Veronica, is up at the*
*door having a fag, blowing smoke out of the open door.*
*Their other sister, Maggie, is up and busy around them,*
*topping up drinks and clearing away plates – as she is*
*through most of this scene. They're all dressed in black*
*and talking ten to the dozen. Much alcohol has been drunk,*
*especially by Jack. Maggie and Veronica are laughing.*

**Jack** She did, she did.

**Eric** It never happened.

**Jack** I remember it as clear as day.

**Maggie** Can you imagine?

**Jack** She'd be there at playtime. She'd lean in against the
railings, coat open, slip her tit through the bars . . .

*Veronica and Maggie laugh more.*

**Veronica** (*miming*) Just lobbed it out!

**Eric** Stop it now.

**Jack** You'd run up and she'd breastfeed you through the
railings.

15

**Eric** She did not. I did not.

**Jack** No one really knew what she was up to. It was all hidden by the tweedy coat. But we knew. You were the golden child and she couldn't bear to see you go.

**Eric** It's just one of those stupid stories.

**Veronica** I remember. I do.

**Maggie** I can't remember anything.

**Jack** She didn't do it for long. She stopped when you were about thirteen.

*They all laugh. Veronica finishes her cigarette, throwing it out of the open door. She shuts the door and joins the others at the table.*

**Eric** (*a touch serious*) I don't wanna hear about it ever again.

*The others are still giggling as Barb, a woman, all dressed in black, even a hat enters. They straighten their faces. Jack tries to hide his laughter with a cough.*

**Barb** I just thought I'd come and say me goodbyes. I've gotta be off.

**Maggie** Aah, have you?

**Barb** Aah yeah, but I'm so glad I could make it. Wasn't it lovely, eh?

**Veronica** It was.

**Barb** Don't take this the wrong way but that has to be one of the best funerals I've been to in a long time. And I've been to a lot.

**Jack** (*aside*) I can imagine.

**Barb** Wasn't it, eh?

**Eric** We know how to do a funeral.

**Barb** You do. She would have loved it. The service. The priest. Wasn't he lovely, eh? What he said. You could tell he really knew her. You know when you go to these ones and you can tell he's never met them. He got what he's saying off the internet.

**Veronica** Yeah.

**Barb** I will miss . . . (*Grasping for the name.*)

**Maggie** Lottie.

**Barb** Lottie. Aah. And the hymns. You had to stick 'I Watch the Sunrise' in, didn't you? Always gets me.

**Veronica** It was one of her favourites.

**Barb** But that's what you want, don't you? (*Almost fighting back the tears.*) A bit of a sob? Lovely. And the spread back here. Look at all this wonderful food.

*A slight pause hangs in the air as she looks at the food.*

**Maggie** Have you had some?

**Barb** Oh no, I'm fine.

**Maggie** There's loads here. Now take some. It won't all get eaten.

**Barb** I couldn't, really.

**Maggie** It'll only go to waste.

**Barb** If you insist.

*Maggie wraps up some sandwiches and sausage rolls in tin foil.*

It won't be the same round here without her. She was the heart and soul of this neighbourhood. And such a lovely family. She brought you up so well. So glad I could make it.

*Barb makes her way round saying her goodbyes. She gives Veronica a kiss.*

Well. Ah, great to see you again.

**Veronica** Yeah, you too. See you.

**Barb** (*kissing Jack*) Tara then. So good to see you.

**Jack** See you.

**Barb** (*seeing that Maggie is near the fairy cakes*) Go on, chuck in a couple of fairy cakes too. Terrible sweet tooth.

*Maggie throws in some fairy cakes.*

Ah thanks. (*Kissing Eric.*) Tara then. You take care.

**Eric** Yeah.

**Maggie** (*looking at the sideboard covered in bottles and cans*) And there's all this booze here too.

**Barb** Go on. I'll take a couple of cans off you then.

*Maggie puts it all in a bag and hands it to her.*

**Maggie** There you go.

**Barb** (*kissing Maggie*) Ah thanks. See you, love.

**Maggie** Thanks for coming.

*Barb heads out. Pause. They all sit in silence for a beat.*

Who was she?

**Jack** Fucked if I know.

*They all start laughing.*

**Eric** You're joking?

**Veronica** (*to Maggie*) I thought you knew her.

**Maggie** Never seen her before in me life.

**Jack** She didn't even know me mother's name. 'I'll miss . . .' *Looking round the room for a card or something with her name on.* And she's taken most of the food and drink with her.

**Eric** You gave it to her.

**Maggie** Cheeky beggar.

**Jack** Who the hell was she?

**Veronica** Professional mourner. Ambulance chaser. They just hang round the cemetery and jump in a car going back to someone's house. She got food, drink, a warm and an afternoon out of the house. Cheeky cow.

*Maggie sits down at the table with the others and has a drink. Pause.*

**Jack** It's just us now. Me mum and dad gone. We've had our lives, done all sorts of things. Had kids, some of us, marriages, divorces . . .

**Veronica** Four in your case.

**Jack** Deaths . . .

**Eric** Well, my wife is still alive. I wish she wasn't.

**Veronica** You say what you feel.

**Jack** And it's just like we're these little kids in this house all over again.

**Maggie** You what?

**Jack** I mean, just at this moment in this room. This kitchen where we grew up, hung out. It's like we never left.

**Maggie** Some of us didn't. (*Aside.*) Not for the want of trying.

**Eric** (*to Jack*) I think you've had enough.

**Jack** If only Frances was here we'd have the full set.

**Maggie** Has anyone heard from her? I thought she might come over for her own mother's funeral, but you know what she's like.

**Veronica** I've stopped trying with her.

**Jack** (*to Maggie*) There's only you left now, Peg. D'you know what you're gonna do?

**Maggie** Oh, I don't know.

**Eric** We should talk about the house and everything.

**Maggie** Shall I put the kettle on? Who wants a brew?

*She gets up, fills the kettle and starts making tea. Being busy again.*

**Jack** It feels like only yesterday I'd be out there playing in the yard. Going off on adventures round the streets. (*To Eric.*) Remember we used to go down to Kirkland and Jennings' Bakery?

**Eric** Oh yeah. You couldn't beat their crusty cobs.

**Jack** (*to Maggie and Veronica*) And they had those electric-motored delivery vans? The bakers would work through the night, do their deliveries and then the vans would be back on charge at four o'clock. And me and him'd sneak in the back and eat anything left over.

**Maggie** You've got such a good memory. You remember all the details.

**Jack** (*looking round the kitchen*) I can see me dad sitting in his chair telling us one of his stories. And me mum in her apron getting the tea together.

*He starts crying.*

**Maggie** Eh, come on now. (*Taking his glass away.*) No more for you.

*Maggie comforts him. He gets himself together quite quickly.*

*Josie, Veronica's daughter, comes through with her boyfriend Simon.*

**Josie** Is there any more whisky? Auntie Pru's practically necking it from the bottle in there.

**Eric** She's not, is she?

**Veronica** There'll be no moving them tonight. She'll be singing soon.

*Maggie finds some more booze in the cupboard.*

**Jack** And who's this? Don't be frightened, lad. We don't bite. Some of us don't.

**Josie** This is Simon. Me new fella.

**Simon** Hiya, really good to meet you all. Sorry it's at such a bad time.

**Josie** You've met me mum.

**Veronica** (*under her breath to Maggie*) He's posh.

**Simon** I'm not posh.

**Veronica** He's from the Wirral.

**Eric** That's posh.

**Simon** Have you been to Birkenhead?

**Veronica** (*to Maggie*) He's handsome though, isn't he?

**Josie** Mother. This is me Uncle Eric and me Uncle Jack.

**Simon** Pleased to meet you.

*He shakes their hands.*

**Eric** Hiya, son.

**Jack** Alright, lad.

**Eric** You can just call me Eric. You're a bit old to be still calling me Uncle Eric.

**Josie** You'll always be me Uncle Eric. And this is me Auntie Maggie. Or Margie as I call her.

**Maggie** Hiya, love.

**Simon** Oh, hi.

*He comes in to kiss her, she not expecting it, and they almost bang heads.*

Went to kiss you but headbutted you instead, sorry.

**Maggie** Nearly knocked me out.

**Simon** I never met your mother, so I feel a bit . . . coming to her funeral, but Josie said I should.

**Maggie** Ah, for the support.

**Jack** For the piss-up more like. Let's get you a drink. What d'you want, son?

**Simon** I'd love a cup of . . .

**Jack** You need something stronger than that. Brandy? Whisky?

**Simon** Maybe a little whisky.

**Jack** A little whisky.

*Jack gets a glass and pours the largest little glass of whisky you've ever seen.*

**Simon** (*taken aback*) Thanks.

*Jack retrieves his glass and tops it back up. Simon takes in the room.*

It's an incredible place you've got here. The house is beautiful. Is it Georgian? Victorian?

**Maggie** I wouldn't know.

*Eric gets up and makes himself a drink. He watches Simon as he does so, slightly unsure of him.*

**Simon** And the street. It's like something off a postcard or out of Dickens.

**Eric** They film loads of your Dickens and period shite round here all the time.

*Josie goes up to Maggie and takes her under her wing as she speaks:*

**Josie** Auntie Margie has lived here all her life.

**Eric** Well, we all did.

**Veronica** She was born in the parlour through there. On the rug in front of the fire.

**Simon** In the middle of the city with all this history round you. (*He looks out of the back window.*) Is that the pub, The Cracke, out the back there?

**Josie** Yeah, yeah. (*To Maggie.*) That's where we first met. He's studying history at the university round the corner, so he loves it round here.

**Jack** University? You see, he is posh.

**Maggie** Have you had anything to eat? Let me put some stuff on a plate for you.

**Simon** I'm not that . . .

*She starts putting some food on a plate for him, working her way round the table.*

**Maggie** It's got to be eaten.

**Simon** The buildings round here. The cathedrals alone, just out the door.

**Veronica** (*to Josie*) You know me mother wanted her service to be at the cathedral. She felt like she practically built the place.

**Maggie** We did ask, but you have to be a pope or Paul McCartney or someone.

**Simon** The Catholic one?

**Josie** Oh God yeah.

**Veronica** She never stepped foot inside the Proddy one.

**Jack** She had a collection box for the new cathedral. Was just over there. It was working-class families that paid for it, you know.

**Eric** (*to Jack*) Is it time for you to get your soapbox out?

**Veronica** We had a missionary box too, which Father Frank would come and collect every Friday night.

**Jack** We had no food in our bellies but the missionary box was always full.

**Eric** (*directed at Veronica*) If someone hadn't had a go at the lock and tried to steal any of it.

**Veronica** Why did I always get the blame?

**Eric** Because it was you.

**Jack** You were obsessed with money.

**Josie** Still are.

**Eric** Me dad hated the church, especially the cathedral. He wouldn't step foot inside the place.

**Jack** What was that all about?

**Maggie** The rows they used to have about the church.

*Maggie is adding the last bits of food to a mountain of food on a plate as she knocks a tea cup over on to the floor. It smashes.*

24

Bugger.

*She cleans it up.*

**Veronica** She's always knocking things over. Let me . . .

**Maggie** It's fine now. I've got it.

**Eric** Ever since she was a kid. Empty room, one glass in the middle of it. Our Maggie will knock it over.

**Maggie** Just get all fingers and thumbs.

*She hands Simon a huge mound of food on a plate.*

There you go. Is that enough?

**Simon** For the rest of me life? Thanks.

**Jack** (*to Simon*) You haven't got much of an accent. If you really are from Birkenhead? Are you sure you're not posh?

**Josie** This is what me Uncle Jack's like. Just ignore him.

**Simon** I never had a really strong accent and I've studied all over the place. So it's gone a bit weird too.

**Eric** You sound like you're from Birmingham. A Brummie.

**Simon** Do I? You know, it's really fascinating hearing you all talk about growing up round here.

**Josie** (*to Simon*) What did I tell you?

**Jack** Doesn't he get out much?

**Simon** I'd love to hear more if I could.

**Jack** He really doesn't get out much. You not got a telly, lad?

**Simon** I'm doing a PhD in local history . . .

**Jack** There you go. What did I say?

**Maggie** Ooh, a PhD. What is that?

**Simon** A doctorate of philosophy. It sounds much fancier than it is. It just means I'd rather carry on studying than get a job. I think this could be the perfect subject for my thesis.

**Eric** (*to Josie*) What's he talking about?

**Josie** Half the time I don't know.

**Veronica** Shush you two. Go on, Simon.

**Simon** You know, what it was like living here, what with all the history and the changes you must have seen. I could interview local people and all you lot.

**Eric** We're just an ordinary family, son.

**Maggie** No one would wanna know about us.

**Simon** I think they would. My thing is oral history.

**Jack** That's disgusting.

**Maggie** Oral. The history of mouths? That's unusual.

**Simon** It's what comes out of mouths I'm interested in. Stories, but not written down. It's about how they're spoken, told.

**Veronica** Isn't he fascinating?

**Maggie** I've never even heard of that before.

**Simon** It's all about interviewing people and letting them speak. Personal testimony.

**Eric** (*to Maggie*) Are you still with him? Cos I'm not.

**Simon** And I think the Liverpool accent and dialect needs to be heard. It's so peculiar but you really want to listen to it. If you just write it down, it doesn't have the same power.

**Josie** You'll have a field day here. Just me Uncle Jack alone. He's a tour guide round Liverpool, anything you wanna know . . .

**Veronica** And lots you don't

**Josie** He'll tell you.

*Eric's mobile rings in his pocket. He takes it out.*

**Eric** Who's this now? (*He looks at who it is.*) Oh God. (*He answers it.*) What do you want? . . . No, of course I'm not missing you . . . I'm only in the next room . . . Is it time for me to take you home? . . . I think it is . . . No, I'm not bringing the whisky through. (*He ends the call.*) Stupid cow. Don't mind me.

*He takes a big swig of drink.*

**Simon** I did a project in Manchester recently and the people I interviewed didn't open up in the same way that they do in Liverpool.

**Jack** Well . . .

**Josie** Don't get me Uncle Jack started on a whole Liverpool versus Manchester thing. Or the Tories.

**Simon** It's not about that. There's this idea that because a lot of people worked in the mills in Manchester, which were so noisy you couldn't hear, and they'd be at work for twelve hours a day and wouldn't speak. So maybe their oral skills didn't develop so much through lack of use. Some of them did that mouthing thing Les Dawson used to do. You know, where you don't say words but you – (*mouthing quietly*) 'mouth them'.

**Josie** Me mum does that. Whenever she says if someone's – (*mouthing quietly*) 'black'.

**Veronica** Do I?

**Simon** So they could be understood over the noise and maybe that's been passed on. But Liverpool had the docks which were so public and almost a performance. They'd be sitting round a lot waiting for the next ship to come in, so maybe this brought out their creativity in banter and storytelling. Only a couple of generations ago a lot of Liverpool was illiterate. You didn't need to read or write to do these jobs and everyone communicated by speech and story.

**Maggie** Really?

**Simon** A lot of dockers were Irish, or of Irish descent, and there's real tradition of storytelling in Irish culture. Though a lot of Mancunians are from Irish descent too. (*To Maggie.*) I'd love to find out what it's like to live here, in this same house all your life. If you're up for it.

**Veronica** If these walls could talk. I've got tons of stories. I'd love to chat, when d'you wanna meet?

**Eric** Is this really the right time to be asking this?

**Simon** Oh sorry, I . . .

**Eric** We've just buried our mother here.

**Simon** I really didn't mean . . .

**Eric** Now's not the time or the place.

> *Simon opens his mouth to say something just as singing starts from the next room. A couple of drunken voices are singing 'If You're Irish Come into the Parlour'. They listen for a moment. We hear part of the first verse.*

**Drunks** (*singing, off*)
If you're Irish come into the parlour –

**Jack** That's all we need. Anything but 'If You're Irish Come into the Parlour.' (*To Eric.*) It'll be your . . .

**Eric** I'd better go and take her home. I'll see you all later.

*Eric rushes off to the front room.*

**Drunks** (*singing, off*)
– There's a welcome there for you;
If your name is Timothy or Pat,
So long as you come from Ireland,
There's a welcome on the mat . . .

*The singing continues but is less audible.*

**Maggie** Be 'Danny Boy' next.

**Veronica** Someone's even trying harmonies in there.

*Jack looks down the hall to see that Eric's not about.*

**Jack** I've got a great story for you. About when our relatives came over from Ireland.

**Maggie** How many times? It's not even true.

**Veronica** Shush you. (*To Simon.*) You'll like this.

**Jack** This is the only bit of family history we know. So our great-great-grandad came over here from Ireland, you know, to get away from the spud famine. Nothing very surprising there I know. He'd bought tickets to New York and most ships stopped off here on the way. But he was sold a ticket to here under the belief that this was New York. And he believed it.

**Simon** No?

**Jack** He wouldn't hear anything different. No matter how many times he was told. He went to his grave still believing this was New York.

**Veronica** How stupid can you get?

**Jack** He wasn't all there . . .

*Jack carries on talking and gesticulating but we can't hear him. The singing continues louder.*

*A rumble starts under the house. We focus on
Maggie as she looks round the kitchen. Taking in the
room and her brothers and sister.*

*At the open back door a young girl appears, aged
eight. It's a young Maggie. She stands and looks out.
Both Maggies do a nervous wringing action with their
hands at the same time. It's clear it's the young Maggie.
Senior Maggie watches her young self as she comes
into the room and appears to be listening to Jack.*

*Senior Maggie looks out as the rumble and the
singing grow louder, odder and more intense.
Something is brewing. Her breathing becomes heavy,
she looks fearful. It reaches a crescendo. Blackout.*

### SCENE TWO

*Hope Hall – what was to become the Everyman Theatre.
An Irish evangelist, Mr Maguire, stands in front of his
flock. The sound of sobbing and crying in among the
crowd.*

**Mr Maguire** It's invitation time. Who is going to come
down the aisle and confess their sins? Who is ready to
receive Christ into their lives?

*A young pregnant woman, Sarah, tentatively makes
her way down the aisle.*

Come down, my child. Don't be frightened now.

**Sarah** I'm not ready. I'm not ready.

**Mr Maguire** You are, my child.

**Sarah** I'm lost.

*She stands in front of the evangelist.*

**Mr Maguire** Jesus is here for you. He knows your sins.
He can see your shame.

He can see your shame.

**Sarah** Please help me.

*Caption:*

### HERE
### 1838

**Mr Maguire** Jesus is here for you. Do not to yield to Satan. Sit down at the Lord's table as I have done and welcome the Saviour in the house of his friends.

*She starts to cry.*

Let the tears flow. The greatest flow of tears.

**Sarah** Will Jesus take me now? Will he?

**Mr Maguire** He's here. Ready for you, my child. The light is here.

*Mr Maguire prays quietly in a low voice.*

**Sarah** Yes, yes.

*Her eyes open wide almost like she's been shocked. Gasps and crying out from the congregation.*

I have seen the light. I have seen the light.

*She collapses. Blackout.*

### SCENE THREE

*8 Hope Place. Basement kitchen. Modern day.*
*Maggie and Simon sit at the table. Simon takes his notepad out and gets his small digital recorder ready.*

**Simon** Thanks for doing this. Josie said you were happy to do it.

**Maggie** Did she now? I'm not sure at all, you know. I really haven't got anything to say.

31

**Simon** Everyone always says that but then I can't shut them up. Especially round here.

*He places the recorder on the table in between them.*

**Maggie** Didn't you want to speak to the others first? I'm all of a jitter.

**Simon** You've lived here all your life. I thought I'd start with you. This'll record us. It's nothing to worry about. I just want to hear your story.

**Maggie** Story? Which one?

**Simon** Of your life. Find out who you are. About growing up here.

*He presses 'record' on his recorder. She looks at him blank.*

Okay, let me ask you some questions. What's your name?

**Maggie** You what? You know me . . .

**Simon** I know, but just for this. (*He points to the recorder.*) Yeah?

**Maggie** Right. (*Beat.*) My name is . . . My name is Maggie Byrne. Well, Margaret or Maggie. Though I've even been called Margie, Mollie, Peg, Peggy, Rita. Even Daisy. Don't know how you get Daisy. Whichever takes your fancy. Oh, I'm doing this all wrong.

**Simon** No, you're not. This is good. What do you prefer to be called?

**Maggie** I quite like Margaret but no one's ever called me that. It sounds a bit grand.

**Simon** Okay, Margaret.

*She smiles.*

And where were you born?

**Maggie**  Well, here.

**Simon**  And where's that? (*Quietly.*) For the tape . . .

**Maggie**  Oh yeah.

*She leans forward and speaks it very clearly into the recorder.*

8 Hope Place, Liverpool. L1 9BG.

*She sits back again.*

**Simon**  And where do you live now?

**Maggie**  I'm still here.

*Simon gestures for her to say more.*

Of course.

*She leans forward again.*

At 8 Hope Place, Liverpool . . . (*Quiet.*) Do you want the postcode again?

**Simon**  It's up to you.

**Maggie**  I'll leave it. You've already got that.

**Simon**  Have you lived here all your life?

**Maggie**  Yeah, yeah. I did almost move away once but it never happened . . .

**Simon**  Can I ask why?

**Maggie**  You don't wanna know about that.

**Simon**  Right, okay. Can I ask what it was like growing up here?

**Maggie**  Fine.

*He gestures for her to say more.*

Right, yes. It was . . . fine. (*Starting to get tangled.*) I've said that. I don't know. It was okay.

**Simon** What's your earliest memory?

**Maggie** Let me think.

*A low rumbling starts that only Maggie can hear. She looks round slightly panicked.*

First memory. (*She thinks, to herself.*) Not that.

*Pause as she thinks.*

**Simon** It can be anything. Doesn't have to be big or significant.

**Maggie** I want something good for you. Me mind's just gone blank.

**Simon** Don't worry. We can come back to . . .

**Maggie** Oh ee ah, I know. Our Jack tells a story of me breaking his train set. Only a little wooden one. I was so clumsy.

**Simon** Is that his memory or your memory?

**Maggie** I think I remember it. (*She thinks.*) I hadn't thought of it like that.

**Simon** It's something I'm interested in. Where memories come from. Family myths.

**Maggie** Shouldn't I have said that? D'you wanna rewind?

**Simon** No, no, it's okay.

*He looks at his notes. He's getting a bit flustered now.*

What was I . . .? Have you got any brothers and sisters? (*Quiet.*) I may ask you things I know, just for the . . .

**Maggie** Yeah, I have.

*He gestures for her to elaborate.*

There's me. Our Eric . . . Then . . . (*She thinks.*) What's she called? Gone blank again.

**Simon** Who, sorry?

**Maggie** Me sister. You've met her. Veronica, Veronica. As if I could ever forget her. I'm sorry. Veronica, our Jack, then Frances . . . And . . .

**Simon** Five?

**Maggie** Yeah, five.

**Simon** What was that like?

**Maggie** It was . . . Well, you don't know anything different do ya.

*She is deep in thought. She looks troubled. It unsettles Simon. Pause.*

**Simon** You happy to continue?

**Maggie** I think so . . .

**Simon** If you're not, then we . . .

**Maggie** You're here now, let's . . .

**Simon** And your parents. Can you tell me about them?

**Maggie** Me mother was called Lottie, Charlotte, and he was . . . Richard. Me dad was called Richard.

**Simon** And what are your memories of them? What were they like?

*Maggie thinks. Pause.*

**Maggie** They were . . . me mum and dad. I've never really thought what they were like. Maybe I should have . . . Me mother's just died . . . So . . .

**Simon** I'm sorry, I shouldn't have . . .

**Maggie** It's fine.

*Simon flicks through his notes.*

**Simon** And you don't own the house? If you don't mind me asking.

**Maggie** Oh no, we – I rent it. Always have. Was off the council, now this housing association thing.

**Simon** It's quite an amazing house for a . . .

**Maggie** I suppose so. It's been in the family for . . . Me mother's mother lived here first and then we . . .

**Simon** What was I going to . . .? (*Looking at his notes.*) Have you worked?

**Maggie** Not really. I've cleaned for people.

**Simon** That's a job. Can you tell me about cleaning?

**Maggie** Like what? About mopping and hoovering?

**Simon** Who have you cleaned for?

**Maggie** Everyone. You don't wanna hear this. Various priests and bishops, a couple of doctors on Rodney Street . . .

*He gives her a thumbs-up to continue.*

Who else? (*She gets herself in a bit of a tangle.*) Why can't I think? I'm being stupid.

*Josie sneaks in with an old shoebox in her hands.*

**Josie** Am I interrupting?

**Simon** (*to Maggie*) Don't worry. That was good. Let's leave it for now.

*He presses 'stop' on his recorder. The rumbling fades out.*

**Maggie** I'm so sorry.

**Simon** It's a difficult time. Your mum's not been long . . . (*Quiet, just to Maggie.*) And I haven't done much of this before myself. I'm still finding my way.

**Maggie** I'll . . .

*She gets up and puts the kettle on.*

(*To Josie.*) I'm no good at it. I did it all wrong.

**Simon** You didn't. You did well, Maggie, Margaret.

**Josie** Margaret? What you calling her that for?

**Maggie** What little brain I've got isn't working.

**Josie** Maybe this will help you. Look.

*Josie opens the shoebox on the table which is full of
old photos. Simon makes some notes in his notebook.*

**Maggie** Where did you find them?

**Josie** In a cupboard upstairs with some of me nan's stuff.
(*Half to Simon.*) I love this house. I used to get so excited
coming here as a kid. From our boxy semi in West Derby
to a house with four floors. A basement. It was like a
castle to me. Something out of a fairy tale. You could
play hide and seek for hours. With Lola the oldest cat in
the world hissing at you from under the stairs. The real
fire in the front room in the parlour. (*To Maggie.*) Didn't
me nan work at a sweet factory? Or have I made that up?

**Maggie** Yeah, Barker and Dobson.

**Josie** She had that cupboard next to the fire full of big
jars of sweets. She'd let you help yourself. Everton Mints,
bon-bons, peardrops. A kid's dream. You'd eat the sweets
and throw the wrappers in the real fire. I don't know
what was more exciting, throwing the wrapper on the
fire or the actual sweet.

**Simon** I should have kept recording.

**Maggie** You see. Ask her, even she knows better than me.

*Josie sees some books on the table next to the
shoebox. She has a nose.*

**Josie** Rome guide, Paris, Valencia . . . You planning a trip?

**Maggie** Naah, just got them out of the library.

**Josie** You been to any of these places?

**Maggie** I've never been anywhere.

*Josie takes out some photos and looks at them. Simon looks too. Maggie makes the tea and half peers over her shoulder.*

**Josie** Look, they were taken here. Is that me mum there?

**Maggie** Yeah. No, it's me. But I've got her beaver on. Now, I do remember that.

**Josie** You what?

**Maggie** Your mother had a beaver coat. Well she thought it was beaver but it wasn't. It was badger or otter or squirrel or something.

*Josie picks out another photo. She shows it to Maggie.*

**Maggie** Your Uncle Jack and Eric, by The Pilgrim.

**Josie** They must be about eight and nine. So cute. Little tearaways.

**Simon** Isn't it great to have actual photos in your hand, rather than two thousand on your phone that you never look at?

**Josie** (*showing Maggie a photo*) Who's that?

**Maggie** That's . . . your grandad.

**Josie** (*to Simon*) He died before I was born.

*Maggie drifts off in thought for a moment. The low rumbling starts. Simon and Josie are oblivious as they look through the photos.*

Ah, me nan there. Has anyone ever done our family tree?

**Maggie** Who'd want to do that?

**Josie** I thought I would. It was Simon's idea.

**Simon** It sounds like there might be some interesting stories back there.

**Josie** I'd love to find out where we all came from. All we know is that New York story.

**Maggie** Hmm, yeah.

*She drifts off again in thought. The rumbling continues. Jack enters through the front door. There's some foreign tourists in bright clothes behind him making a bit of a hubbub.*

**Jack** (*to the tourists*) So this is the actual house I grew up in. Me and Ringo Starr used to sit on this doorstep and have a sing-song. Snap away. I'll just see if anyone's in.

*He heads downstairs.*

Peg?

*Some of the tourists come inside to take photos and pose in the doorway.*

**Maggie** What's all that? Jack?

*He comes down into the kitchen. The rumbling subsides.*

**Jack** Hiya, Peg, kids. I'm just in the middle of a tour with a load of Yanks. I told them that I grew up here. (*To Simon, who's nearby.*) Which is the truth for once. I usually tell them I've lived everywhere. They wanna see inside. You don't mind, do you?

**Maggie** Of course I do.

*Some of the tourists come along the landing and start coming down the stairs.*

**Jack** Ah Peg, I'll slip you a . . .

*Maggie goes to the bottom of the stairs.*

**Maggie** They're coming down the stairs! Jack . . .

**Josie** (*to Maggie*) I'll get rid of them. (*To Jack.*) Come on, out. (*To Maggie.*) We're getting off anyway. (*To Simon.*) We're going out. We'll see you later.

*Josie quickly puts the photos back in the shoebox and puts the lid on. She leaves it on the table. She heads out after Jack and the tourists.*

**Simon** Oh, are we? I was going to do more . . . Oh well, see you later, Margaret. Thanks for the . . .

*Simon rushes out after Josie.*

**Josie** (*to tourists*) Come on, all out.

**Jack** Change of plan.

**Josie** (*to a nosy tourist*) It's only a toilet. No, Ringo didn't use it. Out.

*Maggie takes a deep breath. It's all getting too much. She looks back over at the shoebox. She sits down and opens it. The rumbling starts again. She takes out a couple of photos and looks at them.*
   *Young Maggie, eight, appears next to her at the table and looks at the photos. Senior Maggie watches open-eyed – it's like she's conjured her up from the photo. Young Maggie really studies the photos.*

**Young Maggie** (*shouting through to someone in the larder*) Did me Uncle Douglas take these on his Box Brownie?

*No answer.*

Is that really what I look like?

*Young Jack and Young Eric come in through the back door. Jack has cut his hand.*

40

**Young Eric**  Where's me mum?

**Young Jack**  Don't tell her.

**Young Maggie**  What have you done now? Let me have a look.

**Young Jack**  Shush. It's his fault.

*Young Maggie looks at his cut hand. She takes him over to the sink and starts to clean him.*

**Young Maggie**  How did you do this?

*Lottie, Maggie's mother, comes out of the larder carrying a wrapped-up and sleeping baby, with some vegetables in her other hand. She's busy making the tea.*

**Lottie**  (*seeing Jack's hand*) What have you done now? What's today's injury?

**Young Maggie**  Just a little cut. He'll live.

*She bandages his hand.*

**Lottie**  Is there anything I should know? Are the police gonna be round here again?

**Young Jack**  Naah. Course not.

*Young Veronica comes through the back door in a pretty dress. She dances round the kitchen and sings to herself.*

**Young Veronica**  (*singing*)
The big ship sails on the alley alley O,
Alley alley O, alley alley O . . .

*The front door opens. Young Maggie hears this and looks up towards the door. Richard, the father, enters and heads downstairs. Young Maggie listens and waits for him to appear, anxious to see what he'll be like today.*

The big ship sails on the alley alley O,
On the last day of September.

*She dances off into the house in a world of her own.*
*Richard enters the kitchen but doesn't greet anyone.*
*He heads to the armchair, sits down and reads the*
*paper. He brings in an atmosphere with him.*
*Young Maggie finishes bandaging Jack's hand.*

**Young Maggie** There you go. Be mended in no time.

**Young Jack** Eh Dad, can we down the river this weekend
and look at the ships?

**Lottie** Leave your dad alone. He's just got in from work.

*Young Maggie looks over to her father. The rumbling*
*grows.*
*Senior Maggie quickly puts the photos away in the*
*box and shuts the lid. All the characters from the past*
*disappear.*

*Blackout.*


### SCENE FOUR


*We catch glimpses of Simon's interviews with local*
*residents. We don't see him.*

**Craig** Yeah. I own two bars down in the Albert Dock.
And now we're taking over what was the blind school.
You know, on the corner there opposite the Phil. We're
gonna turn it into a bar, restaurant and night club.
Amazing building it is. It was the blind school, a police
station and the trade unions were there too. It's got all
those little sculptures outside, of what they, the blind,
used to do there. Basket weaving, making brushes and
something to do with pianos. We're gonna keep all them.
It's gonna be amazing.

Me mam was from round here. Lived on Bedford Street. She was a moneylender. Used to help anyone out with a few pennies till the end of the week. She was always fair, but you wouldn't wanna get on the wrong side of her. I was scared of her and she was me mam! We sort of followed her, in a roundabout way. I got into security in clubs and other ways of earning money. If you know what I mean. It's all above board now. Very respectable. Left all that behind. Me two brothers weren't so lucky. They're both in Strangeways. (*Beat.*) Maybe take that last bit out. I wanna be proper now, not bringing all the past back up now, I've moved on. It's taken me long enough.

**Minkie** I've lived on Hope Place for nearly a year now. I'm a producer on BBC Breakfast over in Salford. We got a transfer up from London. We were reluctant at first, to move out of London, not to come here, but once we weighed it all up . . . They paid us a relocation fee, they were very keen for us to come . . . And we were looking for somewhere bigger. Our two-bedroom flat in Stoke Newington was feeling far too small now we had the boys. And what we've ended up with for the money, this beautiful house, I still can't quite believe it. Takes forty minutes to drive across to Salford. You've got some I'm working with who are still doing a commute from London, or half-week there, half-week here. Madness.

My grandfather was from Liverpool, we came here as children, so I do feel a connection. The children love it up here. We actually let them play out in the street, which they can't believe. I haven't really got to know the neighbours yet. There's a woman in her sixties opposite who's lived here all her life. I met her the other day, I was with the boys, she said it's so nice to hear children playing in the street again. Some of these houses were apparently council houses. Can you believe that? I love the street. It'll look so sweet at Christmas.

## SCENE FIVE

*8 Hope Place. Basement kitchen. Modern day.*
*Maggie is drying dishes at the sink. Veronica enters*
*with Josie, both weighed down by boxes. They place*
*them on the dining table.*

**Veronica** There's some lovely stuff up there.

**Josie** She was a right hoarder, wasn't she? What d'you
reckon to this?

*Josie takes out a fancy hat and puts it on.*

**Veronica** It was made for you.

*She practically rolls up her sleeves and starts rooting*
*through the boxes.*

Let's see what's in here then.

*Jack and Eric come downstairs carrying boxes too.*

**Maggie** Don't be bringing more stuff down here.
Whatever you want just take it. I don't want any of it.

**Jack** There must be some things you'd like.

**Maggie** It's all just clutter.

**Jack** Isn't it a bit soon to just get rid?

**Maggie** I've gotta live with it all.

**Veronica** You don't have to live here.

**Maggie** What does that mean?

**Eric** We do need to talk about that. What's happening
with the house?

**Maggie** I don't know. Is something happening?

**Eric** You know about maybe buying it.

**Maggie** I can't afford to buy it.

**Eric** We should all buy it between us. Do it once and for all. You'll be the only one who'll be able to buy it, cos it's registered in your name.

**Maggie** Well . . .

**Veronica** We should have done this years ago. We could have bought it for ten grand in 1986.

**Josie** Wouldn't it be nice to keep it in the family?

**Veronica** Or even not, we'd make a profit on it. D'you know how much these go for now?

**Josie** I'm sure *you* do.

**Eric** Speak to the housing association. Because you've been here so long you get a *sixty* per cent discount.

**Veronica** Sixty? They're practically giving it away. And they won't chuck you out cos of this bedroom tax thing?

**Maggie** Not if you're over sixty. The only benefit of being old and decrepit.

**Jack** It's a disgrace that bedroom tax. The neediest paying for the mistakes of the richest. They're the ones that got us in this mess.

**Eric** (*to Veronica*) Why did you have to mention the bedroom tax?

**Jack** I've never agreed with selling off council houses. I could have done it meself, bought mine in the past, but it's just not right.

**Veronica** I think you're the only person left in the country who's still against it.

**Josie** I love it when me Uncle Jack gets all political.

**Maggie** I just wanted it clearing out. Not all this bringing down.

*No one listens as Jack goes into one of his customary rants.*

**Jack** Where do all the people who need homes go, eh? There's no houses left now. It made us all into a nation of homeowners. Mini-capitalists. All driven by greed and envy.

**Veronica** Is the lecture over yet?

**Jack** The whole economy growing on over-inflated house prices and look where that got us. It's disgusting.

**Eric** Listen, if we buy it, do you wanna be part of it or not? Cos we can do it without you.

**Jack** Oh okay, go on then.

**Eric** (*to Maggie*) So, what you need to do is . . .

**Maggie** Will you stop badgering me? Can I decide what I want to do?

**Eric** Yeah, but . . .

**Veronica** Just to say, I'd love the clock and the Welsh dresser if no one else minds.

**Josie** You can't take stuff and then sell it on.

**Veronica** As if I'd do that.

**Josie** You sell everything else. Put something down for two seconds and you've got it on eBay.

**Jack** (*casual*) Put the kettle on will you, Peg?

*Maggie does as she's told and makes tea. Jack and Eric sit at the table. Josie and Veronica rummage through, getting more and more stuff out. Veronica pulls out a big fur coat. She puts it on Josie.*

**Josie** It's not? Is this the legendary beaver coat?

**Veronica** I thought this was thrown out years ago.

46

**Eric** Still stinks.

**Jack** And it's still not beaver.

**Josie** It is lovely and warm. Look at me beautiful beaver.

**Jack** Eh, stop that.

**Josie** I think it could be real. Feel it. Stroke me beaver.

**Jack** That's enough now.

**Josie** It's boiling hot though.

*Eric's phone rings in his pocket. They all look to him.*

**Eric** Just ignore it.

*The phone continues to ring. Josie takes the coat off and gets out her laptop and a file from her bag. Veronica continues to take odds and sods out of the boxes, making a mess.*

**Josie** (*to Maggie*) Have you got broadband? The internet. (*Scrolling through the wi-fi list.*) Any of these your wi-fi?

*Eric's phone stops ringing.*

**Maggie** Oh yeah, me and your nan were always on the world wide web.

**Josie** Never mind. So, I'm getting some good stuff on the family-tree front.

*Jack's phone starts ringing. He takes it out and looks at it.*

**Jack** (*to Eric*) It's your house. It'll be your Pru.

**Eric** Don't answer it.

**Maggie** What if it's an emergency?

**Eric** It won't be. It never is. I'd be happy if it was. Fallen down a well or the house on fire and her trapped in the back bedroom.

*Jack's phone stops ringing.*

**Josie** Everyone's got the same names. All Marys, Williams, Patricks and Catherines and dead interesting jobs. Coopers, shipbuilders, shoemakers, bottlemakers. Now it'd be all Cheryls and Chanices and call centre, Asda or dole, dole, dole.

**Veronica** She's addicted. It's all she goes on about.

**Jack** Ah, isn't it great to have her back. (*To Josie.*) Is that it now? You done with all your travelling?

**Josie** There's still a few more places I want to see. South America, India and I loved hanging out with our Karen and Natalie and the kids over in Oz. I'm definitely going back there.

**Veronica** She needs to find a proper job, earn some proper money.

**Josie** I'm happy just working in the bar.

**Veronica** Don't get me started on that Alma De Cuba. Turning a perfectly good church into a Brazilian knocking shop.

**Eric** Me mother never got over that. (*To Josie.*) You know, she got married there. Me and him were altar boys.

**Josie** (*heard it a million times before*) I know, I know. (*To Veronica.*) And it's not a knocking shop. It's just a bar. Better to use it than it sit empty. You don't even go to church any more anyway.

**Maggie** I think it's quite nice what they've done to it.

**Veronica** (*to Josie*) And I haven't heard from Simon for me interview. I've been sitting waiting by the phone but not a dickie bird.

**Josie** He'll be in touch.

**Veronica** He's got class. I do like a bit of class.

**Josie** He loved all you lot, couldn't stop going on about you and this house. He's got so much to say. I could listen to him all day. Better than all the scallies round here.

**Veronica** They say opposites attract. You like his brains and he . . . clearly likes a bit of rough.

**Josie** Mother!

**Jack** (*putting his arm round Josie*) How can you say that about my gorgeous niece?

*The house phone starts ringing down the hall. Maggie heads down the hall to answer it.*

**Eric** There's no escape from her. Don't answer it.

**Maggie** It might be someone else.

**Eric** It'll be her or someone from Mumbai trying to sell you something you don't want.

**Josie** There's so much on the internet. I'm on this website where you make your own family tree. Then other people can see if they're related and add themselves. And look, you put things to one side in your 'shoebox' just like you keep old mementos in a real shoebox. I tell you one of the best sites, the Mormon one. They're well into it, you know, because they're looking for the direct descendent of Jesus.

*The house phone stops ringing.*

**Jack** We must have a Jesus in there somewhere.

**Maggie** (*seemingly half throwaway, while making tea*) Are any of you really interested in this?

**Veronica** Oh yeah.

**Jack** I had this bloke from the Wirral on one of me tours the other week. He was telling me they took some of his DNA and he's only related to the Vikings. Can you believe it? I know there's some strange ones over there but a fucking Viking!

**Josie** (*to Jack*) You're not gonna like this. Brace yourself. We've got Tories in the family. And not just sympathisers but a couple of actual councillors.

*Eric and Veronica try to keep in their laughter.*

**Jack** You're joking? You could have told me anything. Murderers, Nazis, Man U supporters. But not Tories.

**Veronica** (*pointing at Eric*) It must be where he gets it from.

*Veronica's mobile rings.*

**Jack** For crying out loud.

**Eric** Imagine how I feel. Give it me.

*Veronica passes Eric her mobile phone. He takes it and walks down the corridor towards the stairs. He goes off.*

(*Off.*) What do you want, woman?

**Veronica** What are your old mates at the *Socialist Worker* gonna say when they hear this?

**Josie** Simon says Liverpool was a Tory town at one point.

**Veronica** This is what I get all day long, 'Simon says, Simon says . . .'

**Eric** (*off*) Who would I be having an affair with? I can hardly walk never mind anything else.

*Maggie brings a tray of tea and biscuits to the table.*

**Maggie** Right, put all this away.

*She tries to tidy away some of the clothes back into the boxes. Jack takes a biscuit straight away.*

**Veronica** In a minute.

**Maggie** I'll just put it away for you then.

*Maggie starts to shove the bits of clothes back away in the box. Over the top to make her point.*

**Josie** So on me great-grandma's side . . .

**Veronica** We haven't finished there.

**Maggie** Well I have.

**Veronica** Maggie.

**Maggie** If you're not gonna put them away then . . .

*She frantically shoves the stuff away. Eric comes in from the hall with the phone in his hand.*

**Veronica** You're being stupid now.

**Maggie** (*rage from nowhere*) Don't call me stupid! I'm not stupid! (*She starts crying.*) I've had enough of it. I can't take any more. All this crap of hers. And I don't want to know any of this. (*Referring to Josie's family-tree research.*) I don't want to hear about any of it.

*She turns away and cries.*

**Josie** Oh God. I didn't know. I thought . . .

**Veronica** What's got into you?

*Maggie doesn't answer. The words won't come. Pause.*

What is it? Will someone explain to me because as far as I'm concerned I was just . . .

**Eric** (*to Veronica*) Leave it, eh.

**Jack** Always going on.

**Veronica** She's completely overreacting.

**Jack** Have a bit of sympathy.

**Eric** Yeah.

**Josie** Yeah, Mother.

**Veronica** Why's everyone having a go at me?

**Jack** You just make it worse, don't you?

**Veronica** Me? What have I done?

**Jack** Our Peg's upset and you're making it all about you.

**Maggie** Just go.

**Jack** You what?

**Eric** You want us to go?

*She nods.*

**Veronica** I'm outta here. I don't need to stand around to . . .

*She grabs her bag and storms out.*

**Josie** But . . .

**Jack** This is not like you. What about the tea?

*Eric gives Jack a look.*

**Maggie** Please just go.

*Josie gets her things together.*

**Josie** I'm sorry if I've upset you, Auntie Margie.

*She heads out. Jack and Eric head out. Jack takes another biscuit. Eric goes to say something but he doesn't know what to say and heads out. Maggie turns as the rumbling starts. She's almost expecting it.*
*Young Maggie appears and dries the dishes at the sink just as Maggie was. The images are much more splintered. Senior Maggie watches.*
*Lottie comes out of the larder carrying a wrapped-up and crying baby.*

**Lottie** Shush now. What's all this racket?

*She rocks the baby until it stops crying.*

That's better. (*To Young Maggie.*) D'you wanna light the fire when you've done that?

*A very elderly woman, Kitty, appears at the top of the stairs with a stick.*

Mother, is that you?

*Young Jack and Young Eric run through, round the table and up the stairs, playing a game.*

**Young Jack** You're on now.

**Young Eric** No, you.

**Kitty** Maggie. Can you help me?

**Young Maggie** Why don't they do the dishes?

**Lottie** Boys don't do dishes.

*Young Veronica appears from under the stairs.*

**Young Veronica** Lola. Puss, puss.

*She disappears back under the stairs. The front door opens. Young Maggie looks up towards the door. Richard, the father, comes in and heads downstairs. It's like a replay of the earlier moment. Young Maggie listens and waits to see how he'll be. He enters the kitchen and seems much more cheerful today. He sees Maggie drying the dishes.*

**Richard** That's a good girl. What's for tea?

**Maggie** A pie. Chicken pie.

**Lottie** Your favourite.

**Richard** Just what I need.

*He sits down in the armchair.*

(*To Maggie.*) Wanna hear a story? Wanna hear about when I went to New York?

**Maggie** Yes please.

*He signals for her to come over. She rushes over and sits on his lap.*

**Richard** Now, where shall I begin?

*Blackout.*

### SCENE SIX

*We hear more of Simon's interviews.*

**Jack** I'm part of the number one industry in Liverpool now. Tourism. I've always liked a good tale and when I was laid off for the umpteenth time I thought that's it, I'm gonna take control here. I was an engineer but there's none of that round here any more. I do tours of the docks, the Beatles, up here along Hope Street and one of me most popular ones, me ghosts and murder tour. People love a good murder and there's been some cracking ones round here. I often dress up, cos they like that and if it's a spooky one I pay some kid to jump out from behind a gravestone with a sheet over them.

There's loads of tours here now. I know I'm not the most factual, for me it's more about the experience rather than facts and the truth. I want them to go away having heard the best stories and remembering that day for ages. So maybe I might say I sat next to Cilla in school. Or Wayne Rooney's me nephew. I'm not hurting anyone am I?

**Jonathan** I'm a doctor at the Royal. Oncology. Originally from Edinburgh. I live at number forty-seven Hope Street now. There's a funny connection with Edinburgh and me and here. Sort of. You might have heard of Burke and Hare, the grave robbers, from Edinburgh. Well, number forty-seven is where Liverpool's body snatchers lived. Apparently. Eighteen twenty-seven it was. There was a terrible smell coming from the house. They found eleven bodies pickled in brine on the ground floor. And thirty-three babies' bodies, in barrels, in the cellar. They were digging up bodies from the cemetery and selling them on for anatomy lectures. Doctor's needed corpses so . . . Ten pound a body. Which is quite a mark-up.

My wife Jeanette hates the whole idea of it and insists we sleep with the light on What she doesn't know is I picked this house because of that story. Gives the place a bit of colour and I thought it'd be a great story to tell at dinner parties. But she won't even let me mention it. You do get a waft of the strangest smell sometimes and it does send a shiver down my spine but it can't be anything to do with all that. It's not. I know it's not.

**Monica** I've been here about five years. On Rice Street. Just me and me son Ryan, he's six now. We're in a council, well they call it social housing now. Small flat but it's nice. I like it round here, it's, it's quiet. Compared to where we were before. I know it well up here. You said you'd take any names out, yeah? Okay. Yeah, I used to work up here. On the street you know. Just by the Anglican cathedral. I went mad when they gave me this flat cos I was on the straight and narrow and they were sending me right back to where it all started to go wrong. But I've got a job now, in Boots, on the tills. And that keeps me sorted. I see some of the girls I used to know. They're still here. Loads of new young ones though. I can see meself in them. You see I'm dead boring now, if you'd found me three years ago I'd have had much better stories for you. But if I'd carried on the way I was going, I wouldn't be here.

55

## SCENE SEVEN

*Hope Street Picture House – what was to become the Everyman Theatre. It's a Saturday morning cowboy film. We can hear a shoot-out, Red Indians and lots of kids enjoying it. Booing and cheering at the screen. The projection flickers from behind over the tops of their seats. Young Maggie and Veronica enter down the side.*

**Young Veronica** Ah, it's already started.

**Young Maggie** Why did we come in the back door?

**Young Veronica** Cos the blind fella's on the door there and we haven't got any money.

**Young Maggie** But you paid him.

**Young Veronica** Yeah with two buttons.

**Young Maggie** You didn't? That's terrible.

**Young Veronica** He's none the wiser. Shush now, here'll do.

*They both find seats and sit down.*

The westerns are my favourite. Especially when they're violent.

**Young Maggie** I just love getting out the house. I love it here.

*Caption:*

### HERE

#### 1955

*Young Eric appears on one side looking for her.*

**Young Eric** Maggie? Veronica?

**Young Maggie** Duck.

*They duck down, not wanting to be seen.*

**Young Eric** Are you here? Maggie?

**Kid** (*off*) Shut up, will you. I can't hear the Lone Ranger over you.

*Eric disappears. Maggie and Veronica reappear.*

**Young Maggie** Has he gone?

**Young Veronica** Narrow escape. Always trying to ruin our fun.

*Eric appears on the other side of her.*

**Young Eric** There you are. What are you doing in here?

**Young Veronica** What does it look like?

**Young Eric** Maggie, me mum needs you.

**Young Maggie** I'm busy.

**Young Eric** Me dad's drunk again.

**Young Maggie** I'm watching this.

**Young Veronica** Yeah, go away.

**Kid** (*off*) Some of us are trying to watch a film here.

**Young Eric** We don't know what to do.

**Young Maggie** Me mum'll deal with it.

**Young Eric** She's locked herself in the bathroom.

**Kid** (*off*) Can you do this outside?

**Young Maggie** Is she okay?

**Young Eric** I don't know. Please . . .

**Young Maggie** But I'm . . .

**Young Eric** Just come please . . .

**Young Maggie** Okay!

*Maggie heads out with Eric.*

**Young Veronica** I'm staying here.

*Blackout.*

## SCENE EIGHT

**Veronica** I don't know what it is but I've always been
fascinated by money. I love having it. Maybe because
there wasn't much of it about when we were growing up.
That fear of not having it. I've always worked, sometimes
juggling three jobs at once. Me mother had various jobs
too, factories, cook, cleaner. She had to, she couldn't rely
on me dad's wages. He'd get paid on a Friday night, in
the pub, The Ship, that his boss owned. Usually after they
were already half bladdered. And it all just went back
into his boss's pockets, didn't leave the pub. Unless me
mother got there in time. She'd drag us round various
pubs looking for him. I don't know why she took us. If
he wasn't in The Ship we'd be in and out of every pub on
Scottie Road. One on every corner. Someone said there
was seventy of them at one time. And it felt like that.

He was a big drinker, me dad. And even if he hadn't
pissed most of it up the wall, it was never a regular wage
anyway. With the docks you didn't know you were
working from one week to the next. You just turned up
each week and hoped you'd get picked. They call it zero
hours contracts now. (*Beat.*) Me mother had to be creative
in the face of, well, poverty. You had moneylenders,
who'd come door to door. All women. Some hard as
nails, some all sweetness and light. The soft ones would
have their sons with them and wade in if there was any
trouble. Sometimes me mum would be straight down the
pawnbroker's on the Monday morning. Put me dad's suit
in, it'd get you through the week until the wages came in

and you took it back out on the Friday. He was none the wiser. Just like Cash Converters now. Some things don't change.

## SCENE NINE

*8 Hope Place. Basement kitchen. Modern day.*
  *Eric in the kitchen with a man in a sharp suit, Rob, who's taking down the details of the room in a notepad.*

**Rob** Brilliant location.

**Eric** Oh yeah.

**Rob** (*looking at the staircase*) Lovely period details. Great house you've got, Mr Byrne.

**Eric** Ah, thanks.

**Rob** Have you spoken to any other estate agents?

**Eric** No, you're the first.

**Rob** And only. I hope.

  *They both force out a laugh at the same time.*
  *A mobile phone starts ringing.*

**Eric** Not now.

  *Eric searches through his pockets but it's Rob's. He takes out his phone and answers it.*

**Rob** (*into phone*) Hi . . . Yeah . . . I'm here now . . .

**Maggie** (*off*) Hello?

**Rob** (*into phone, half quiet*) Amazing . . . (*Quieter.*) Oh yeah, I'm not letting this one out of me sight . . .

  *Maggie comes downstairs and into the kitchen. She's dressed in her housecoat and is looking quite dishevelled.*

59

**Maggie** I thought I could hear voices. Who's he?

**Eric** Shush.

*Rob ends the phone call.*

**Rob** Are you thinking of putting it on the market soon?

**Eric** Maybe. Depends on the . . .

**Rob** Of course. If I can just have a look upstairs. (*He sees Maggie.*) Hiya.

**Eric** Sure, sure.

*Rob goes up the stairs into the rest of the house.*

**Maggie** What's happening?

**Eric** I just thought it was worth getting the house valued.

**Maggie** But we don't even own it.

**Eric** He doesn't know that.

**Maggie** But . . .

**Eric** Just curious. That's all.

**Maggie** Okay. I'll . . . Tea?

**Eric** Naah. Fine thanks. You're not dressed.

**Maggie** I know.

*She takes a deep breath.*

You know . . . Eric . . .

*She tries to speak but it won't come.*

**Eric** Yeah?

*Maggie goes to speak.*

(*Half to himself.*) Should I show him round or let him look himself? I'll leave him for a minute.

**Maggie** Well . . .

**Eric**  You've got to get dressed. Get up and out. This does nothing for you.

**Maggie**  Do you remember what it was like living here?

**Eric**  Of course. Don't you?

**Maggie**  I do and I don't. I don't know what's real or . . .

**Eric**  (*not really listening*) I don't know what you're talking about.

**Maggie**  Shall I put the kettle on?

**Eric**  You've already asked me that.

**Maggie**  Sorry, sorry.

**Eric**  While I'm here I got the documents to buy the house. (*He takes out some forms.*) We can get the money together, you don't have to worry about that.

**Maggie**  I haven't thought about it.

**Eric**  You don't need to think about it, just sign them. I'll leave them there for you. (*He places them on the table.*) I'd better go and see . . .

*He moves to head upstairs.*

**Maggie**  Eric.

*He stops.*

**Eric**  What is it?

*She wants to say something. She can't find the words. Pause.*

**Maggie**  I'll look at them. The forms.

**Eric**  Great. (*And he's off.*) Tara.

**Maggie**  Tara.

*She's left alone – the rumbling starts.*

*Young Maggie appears dressed in her school uniform. Lottie comes in all dressed in black. She stops still and takes a deep breath.*

**Young Maggie** Do we have to go to school?

**Lottie** Yes.

**Young Maggie** But shouldn't we be there?

**Lottie** You're going to school. You make sure they all go today. (*Beat.*) You said your goodbyes through there?

**Young Maggie** Yeah.

**Lottie** Then off you go. Go on.

**Young Maggie** I want to go to the cemetery too.

**Lottie** I don't wanna hear another word about it. Now get.

*Blackout.*

SCENE TEN

*Eric sits with Simon.*

**Eric** Just so you know, I don't want to be here.

**Simon** Oh, right. Okay.

**Eric** Josie twisted me arm.

**Simon** I promise it won't hurt.

**Eric** I just feel daft. I don't know what I'm going to say.

**Simon** Everyone says that. Let's just give it a go.

*He presses 'record' on his digital recorder.*

So if we start with . . .

**Eric** (*steamrollers in and leans towards the tape*) You have got loads of history round here. I've done me research. You've got The Cracke pub there, where John

Lennon used to go and there's a plaque about him. I've heard the Philharmonic, not the pub, the other place, had something to do with the *Titanic*. And the bogs in the Phil pub are famous too. What else?

**Simon** That's great. Really great. If we just go back a bit.

**Eric** (*quite put out*) Oh. Have I done it wrong?

**Simon** There's no right or wrong but . . .

**Eric** Looks like I have. Tell me what you want, son.

**Simon** I don't want to impose too much but I'd love to maybe hear more about your personal experiences. About what it was like growing up here.

*Eric looks at him blank.*

I'd love to hear about your family, friends, what you ate, where you played . . . Okay, can you tell me your earliest memory?

**Eric** That's not history.

**Simon** It can be.

**Eric** History is the famous stuff. You know, what you do in school. Kings and Queens, Henry the Eighth, Battle of Hastings and all that. Who's going to be reading about what I had for me tea?

**Simon** Well, that's one part of history. I'm interested in the smaller stories, the everyday.

**Eric** But why do that when there's loads of proper history round here?

**Simon** That's what excites me.

**Eric** I knew I shouldn't have come.

*Blackout.*

## SCENE ELEVEN

*8 Hope Place. Basement kitchen. Modern day.*
   *Josie enters the dark kitchen with Veronica from the back kitchen door. The place is looking much emptier. The last of the daylight is disappearing.*

**Josie** She's probably upstairs. She hardly ever goes out. Look.

   *She points to a bowl full of cat food on the floor.*

Cat food. There isn't a cat.

**Veronica** Maybe she's got one.

**Josic** She hasn't. She's been calling it Lola.

**Veronica** That's what our cat was called.

**Josie** Exactly. I think she might be losing it. Seeing things. Imagining there's a cat here. I've been round a few times and she's either locked in her room or looking for this cat.

**Veronica** Where is everything? Has she got rid of more stuff?

**Josie** She put a sign up on the *open* front door saying 'Take whatever you want'. So they did.

**Veronica** Who?

**Josie** Any old weirdo passing by. Luckily I arrived just as two skanks were trying to carry out the fridge.

   *They hear footsteps coming down the stairs.*

Hang on.

**Maggie** (*off*) Puss. Puss.

   *Maggie comes down in her dressing gown looking quite dishevelled and covered in splodges of different coloured paint.*

I want all the keys back. This is my house now, my home.

**Veronica** We've always all had keys.

*She pours more dry cat food into the already full bowl. It spills over the floor.*

I think you've done enough now.

**Maggie** She's hungry. She hasn't eaten for a while.

**Veronica** Is there a cat?

**Maggie** You what?

**Veronica** Is that food for a cat?

*Maggie looks at her like she's mad.*

**Maggie** Is the cat food for a cat? What else do you think it's for? A dog? A donkey? For me? Do you think I'm eating the cat food?

**Veronica** Well no . . .

**Maggie** What a daft question. Have you lost it? (*To Josie.*) Is it her turn to go crazy? (*She starts calling for the cat.*) Puss. Puss. Come on. Dinner time. Lola. (*To Veronica and Josie.*) She often hides under the stairs. (*To cat.*) You coming out?

**Veronica** Remember we had a cat called Lola? Who used to hide under the stairs?

**Maggie** Of course. So what *do* you want?

**Josie** We've just come to see you, Auntie Margie.

**Maggie** Well here I am. I'd make you a cup of tea but I don't do that any more.

**Veronica** Drink tea?

**Maggie** No, wait hand and foot on people. (*Beat.*) What I want to know is, who am I?

**Veronica** Do you not know who you are?

**Maggie** Of course I do. Don't be soft.

**Josie** Then what . . .?

**Veronica** (*pointing to the paint on her dressing gown*) What's all that?

**Maggie** I've been painting.

**Veronica** Why?

**Maggie** Why not? I remembered I loved art at school . . . But I didn't do that for long. I was too busy . . . Shall I show you? I've done a family portrait.

*Maggie heads off to retrieve a canvas at the bottom of the stairs.*

**Veronica** She's had her moments but I've never seen her like this.

**Josie** Is it grief? What should we do? Maybe I could move in for a while . . .

*Maggie enters with a large framed canvas in her arms, the back towards us – we can't see what's on it. She turns it round. There's a collection of figures with realistic looking bodies and dark black splodges for faces. They're all standing round a campfire.*

**Maggie** What d'you think?

**Veronica** Well . . .

**Maggie** I know there's too much red. I'm aware of that.

**Josie** Yeah . . .

**Maggie** It's not finished, of course. That's Eric, Jack, Frances, you. Me mum and dad. Lola. All round a campfire. I'm pleased with the fire.

**Veronica** You're not in it?

**Maggie** Oh no. No way. No way José. (*She looks at the picture.*) Still needs work. Maybe I should include the beaver coat . . .

*Josie giggles. Veronica and Maggie both look at her.*

**Josie** Sorry.

*Maggie puts the picture to one side.*

**Veronica** And is that one of me mum's paintings you've painted over? The lion with the shoulders.

**Maggie** You always hated it and put a sheet over it because it scared you.

**Veronica** Maybe, but still . . .

**Josie** Are you missing me nan?

**Maggie** Nope.

**Veronica** Should we get Dr Wardale?

**Maggie** Are you not well?

**Veronica** No, for you.

**Maggie** What's wrong with me?

**Veronica** Well . . .

**Maggie** I know I've looked better. Haven't combed me hair and this housecoat's seen better days. But if you can't dress like a tramp round your own home then where can you, eh?

*She moves across the room and there's a faint rattling sound.*

What's that noise?

**Josie** I can't hear anything.

*Maggie moves about the room swinging her dressing gown about. There's a rattling noise.*

**Maggie** It's like maracas. It's me. (*She shakes.*) It's all me pills. They're in me pockets of me housecoat. But I reckon if you just shook me I'd make the same noise. I'm so full of pills.

**Veronica** What the hell are you taking?

**Maggie** Same old ones. Didn't you know? You don't really know me. I don't know me. So how would you?

**Josie** Do you think you should be taking pills?

**Maggie** I've been on them for so long I don't know what else to do. This one to make me lie down, that one to make me stand up . . .

*Jack and Eric enter through the back door into the kitchen. Jack is dressed like Sergeant Pepper.*

**Eric** (*to Josie*) I got your message, thought I should come.

**Maggie** Oh they're all here. (*To Jack.*) What the frig have you come as?

**Josie** Yeah, what is that?

**Jack** I've just finished a Beatles' Sergeant Pepper tour. Didn't have time to change.

**Eric** (*to Veronica, quiet*) What's she been saying?

**Veronica** Can't make head nor tail of it.

**Maggie** I can hear you, you know.

**Jack** You alright, Peg?

**Eric** Is there anything we can do for you?

**Maggie** Yes. Actually there is.

*They all look to her.*

I think one of the radiators needs bleeding. Making a
funny noise and doesn't get warm. The one in the front
parlour.

**Veronica** (*disappointed*) Oh.

**Eric** I could do that. (*To Veronica.*) She seems fine.

**Maggie** Fine, fine, fine.

**Eric** (*to Maggie*) Have you had a look at those forms
I gave you?

*He notices them on the table. He looks at them.*

Clearly not. They haven't moved from the spot I left them
in. Hey love, why don't you sign them now?

**Josie** Is now really the time for that?

**Eric** We just get this signed and then it's done.

**Jack** Maybe not now, Eric. (*Quietly.*) Does she even
know what she's signing?

**Eric** (*to Jack*) Do you want this house to stay in our
family or to go to a load of Romanians?

**Veronica** Maggie, sign these forms now!

**Eric** (*to Maggie*) Just a little scribble, here, here and here.

*He hands her a pen. She takes it and is about to sign
when the knocker at the front door goes.*

**Maggie** Oh, here we go. Who else? Uncle Tom Cobley
and all? Frances? All the way from America?

**Veronica** Go and get the door, Josie.

**Josie** Why me?

*Josie heads off upstairs to answer it. Maggie holds the
pen in the air.*

**Maggie** Is this what I want to do?

**Eric** You know it's right.

**Maggie** What's right and what's wrong? Always got to do the right thing or be seen to do the right thing.

**Veronica** Oh, just sign it. It'll only take a minute.

**Jack** It is the right thing, Peg. Go on.

*Maggie thinks for a moment. She decides to sign and is just about to put pen to paper as Josie comes back in with Carla, from the local housing association.*

**Josie** This is Carla. She's from . . .

**Carla** Liverpool Maritime Housing Association. Hello, everyone. Hi. Hiya.

*Her eye is drawn to Jack in his get-up. She doesn't know what to say.*

**Jack** Don't ask.

**Carla** I'm looking for Ms Byrne. Margaret Byrne.

**Maggie** I'm here! Coo-ee.

**Carla** Oh, hiya. I'm not interrupting anything am I?

**Eric** Now's not the best . . .

**Maggie** Not at all. I'd make you a cuppa but I don't do that any more.

**Carla** (*not sure how to respond*) Oh right, okay. We spoke on the phone about you wanting to return the house back to us.

**Veronica** You what?

**Eric** Hang on.

**Maggie** I remember now. What do I need to do?

**Carla** Just sign the withdrawal form. It's quite straight forward.

**Maggie** And I've got a pen here, in my hand. I'm all ready.

*Carla gets some forms out of her bag. Josie starts laughing.*

**Veronica** This is not funny, Josie!

**Josie** Sorry I'm just nervous. I can't believe I'm laughing, sorry.

**Eric** Maggie? What you playing at?

**Maggie** Decided to get rid. Fresh start and all that.

**Jack** Where would you go?

**Carla** We'd rehouse Ms Byrne of course. We're very grateful to get a larger house like this back into our stock. It's almost unheard of. (*A touch excited.*) It's the first time I've overseen one myself and . . .

**Veronica** You can't do this.

**Maggie** (*to Carla*) Can I?

**Carla** Er, yeah.

**Maggie** Okey-dokey.

**Jack** Come on, Peg, why you doing this? Think of the family.

**Maggie** I've thought enough of the family. (*To Carla.*) Whereabouts, Carla?

**Carla** Is there a problem?

**Eric / Veronica / Jack** Yeah.

**Maggie** (*simultaneously*) No.

**Carla** I can come back another time.

**Maggie** Now's perfect.

*Maggie goes to sign. Eric snatches the forms away.*

**Eric** I'm not letting you. You can't.

**Maggie** I can do whatever I want. It's about bloody time I did what I want to do.

**Carla** Excuse me.

*Carla tries to take the form but Eric pulls it away. She snatches at the thin air.*

**Eric** You're going to do as you're told.

**Maggie** And who are you? Bobby Big Bananas?

**Carla** Can I have my withdrawal form back, please?

**Eric** You see, this is our house too.

**Carla** (*looking at a document*) I understood it was only Ms Byrne that lived here.

**Veronica** We did live here.

**Jack** Our whole family lived here.

**Carla** But you don't live here now. You're not down on my form here.

*Eric leads Carla to one side.*

**Eric** (*half whispered*) She's not very well.

**Maggie** I can hear you.

**Eric** Our mother died recently . . . and she's not all with it at the best of times.

**Maggie** No. No! No more. How dare you say that. I'm not the mad one. I am not! Give it here.

*She snatches the forms off Eric, puts them on the table and starts signing.*

There.

*Carla subtly points to another place to sign.*

And there. Done.

*She hands the forms back to Carla.*

**Carla** (*feeling quite awkward*) Well, thanks. That's . . . great. Bye then.

*She sidles out.*

**Eric** Why did you do that?

**Maggie** I don't have to explain myself.

**Veronica** I think you do.

*Maggie doesn't answer. Pause.*

**Josie** Listen, maybe it is up to me, Auntie Margie, to . . .

**Veronica** Don't talk shite, Josie. (*To Maggie.*) Is that it then?

**Jack** That's the end of this house being in our family. Over just like that.

**Eric** We could have turned this into flats. A guest house, hotel.

**Veronica** The revenue you'd have made. Have you got nothing to say?

**Maggie** No. No, I haven't.

**Eric** I'm going to see if we can turn it round. Let me catch her up . . .

*He dashes out after her.*

**Veronica** Good idea. (*To Maggie.*) Crazy. You are crazy. Come on, Josie.

*She heads out. Josie doesn't move.*

**Veronica** Josie!

*Josie follows her mum out.*

**Jack** I don't understand. Peg? D'you wanna talk or . . .?

*Maggie doesn't answer. Jack heads out.*
*Maggie is left alone. It's evening now and dark outside. She sits at the table deep in thought. The rumbling starts again. She starts to breathe heavily. The past fills up the room. Young Veronica runs through.*

**Young Veronica** Coming ready or not.

*Lottie appears from under the stairs.*

**Lottie** It's in the family. It's in the blood. There's always one.

*Young Jack and Young Eric are at the top of the stairs laughing.*
*Maggie looks under the table and spots Young Maggie hiding under there. She's covering her ears. Richard appears. He and Lottie argue either side of the table.*

Look at the state of you.

**Richard** I should have stayed out.

**Lottie** I don't wanna see you like this.

**Richard** I should have ran when I had the chance. Before I was trapped. Before you got pregnant with her. Then there was no escape. New York. I wish I was in New York.

**Lottie** We all wish you were there.

**Young Maggie** (*with her hands over her ears*) Make them stop. Make them stop.

**Maggie** Make it stop. Please make it stop.

*Young Maggie climbs out from under the table and looks to Senior Maggie. Maggie reaches into the pocket of her dressing gown and takes out a bottle of pills. She looks at them, unsure of what to do. She empties them out on to the table. Still unsure.*

**Young Eric** Can we go down the river today, Dad?

**Richard** Just one more drink. A little whisky.

**Young Jack** Eh Peg, don't cry. It's not your fault.

**Young Veronica** (*trying to entice the cat out from under the stairs*) Puss, puss. Lola.

*Maggie takes another bottle out and empties it. And another.*
*Young Maggie goes into a cupboard and finds another bottle. She hands it to Senior Maggie who empties the contents out.*

**Richard** Let me tell you a story.

**Lottie** What's in the cat's in the kittens. Stupid, stupid girl.

**Young Veronica** (*singing*)
The big ship sails on the alley alley O . . .

*Young Jack laughing.*
*Young Maggie finds a pack under the sink. She hands it to Senior Maggie who frantically pops them out of their packet too.*

**Lottie** What's that smell? Is something burning?

**Richard** Not so much a shotgun wedding as a machine-gun wedding.

*Young Maggie finds another pack in the drawer in the table and hands them to Senior Maggie.*

**Lottie** (*crying*) She's not breathing. She's not breathing.

75

*The family fades out.*
  *Maggie looks at the mound of tablets on the table.*
*She pours herself a glass of water and scoops up a*
*handful in her hand. Young Maggie looks at her, then*
*fades into the background. Maggie takes a deep breath.*

**Simon** (*off*) Margaret? Hello? You in?

*He appears at the back window.*

I've just been to The Cracke. Bit too much to . . . I
thought I'd come and say . . .

*He sees Maggie at the table with the tablets. She has a*
*handful of pills in her hand and is about to take them.*

Margaret. Maggie!

*He opens the door and rushes in.*

**Maggie** No more.

**Simon** You can't.

*Simon takes the pills off her and pushes them aside.*

**Maggie** I have to.

**Simon** Please, no, don't . . . I won't let you. Have you
taken any?

**Maggie** I don't think so. But I . . .

**Simon** Oh Margaret . . . What should I . . .? I don't
know . . .

*He's unsure what to do and awkwardly puts an arm*
*round her.*

It's going to be okay . . .

**Maggie** Is it?

*She puts her arms round him and cries deep into him.*
*He awkwardly tries to comfort her.*

**Simon**  Margaret, I'm so sorry.

**Maggie**  Who am I?

**Simon**  I don't know what you . . .

**Maggie**  What's the . . . ? The story . . .

**Simon**  Come on now.

**Maggie**  What's my . . . ?

**Simon**  Did you take any? Should I call a . . . ?

**Maggie**  No, no.

**Simon**  Do you want me to call Veronica? Or Jack or someone?

**Maggie**  They can't help me. Nobody . . .

*She breaks apart and looks at him.*

Can you help me?

**Simon**  If I can . . .

**Maggie**  Can you? What happened? I wanna know.

**Simon**  (*still confused*) Okay.

**Maggie**  It's broken . . . I've got these broken bits of memory.

**Simon**  It's going to be okay, Margaret.

**Maggie**  Where I came from. What's true?

**Simon**  I'll do anything I can.

**Maggie**  (*with renewed urgency*) Please help me. I need to . . . I need to know everything.

*Blackout*

*End of Act One.*

# Act Two

## SCENE ONE

*The atmosphere of a very rowdy music hall – that was to become the Everyman Theatre.*

*A middle-aged, old-mother-type singer, Lily Lloyd, gets up. The first two songs should be performed as the audience are coming back after the interval.*

**Lily** (*singing*)
Has anybody here seen Kelly?
K-E-double-L-Y.
Has anybody here seen Kelly?
Find him if you can.
He's as bad as old Antonio,
Left me on my own-ee-o,
Has anybody here seen Kelly?
Kelly from the Isle of Man.

(*Speaking.*) Here's a good 'un.

(*Singing.*) She's a lassie from Lancashire,
Just a lassie from Lancashire,
She's the lassie that I love dear,
Oh, so dear.
Though she dresses in clogs and shawl,
She's the prettiest of them all.
None could be fairer or rarer than Sarah,
My lass from Lancashire.

(*Speaking.*) Shall we have another?

(*Singing.*) Mrs Moore, who lives next door,
Is such a dear old soul,
Of children she has a score,
And a husband on the dole!
I don't know how she manages to keep that lot I'm sure,

I said to her today as she was standing at the door:

'Don't have any more, Mrs Moore,
Mrs Moore, please don't have any more!
The more you have the more you'll want, they say,
And enough is as good as a feast any day.
If you have any more, Mrs Moore,
You'll have to take the house next door.
They're alright when they're here,
But take my advice, old dear,
Don't have any more, Mrs Moore!'

*The audience should all be in now and the second act proper begins.*

(*Speaking.*) You all back in now? Let's have one more before we crack on.

(*Singing.*) I'm in a nice bit of trouble, I confess;
Somebody with me has had a game.
I should by now be a proud and happy bride,
But I've still got to keep my single name.
I was proposed to by Obadiah Binks
In a very gentlemanly way;
Lent him all my money so that he could buy a home,
And punctually at twelve o'clock today –

*Caption:*

### HERE

### 1892

**Lily** (*singing*)
There was I, waiting at the church,
Waiting at the church,
Waiting at the church;
When I found he'd left me in the lurch,
Lor, how it did upset me!
All at once, he sent me round a note
Here's the very note,
This is what he wrote:

'Can't get away to marry you today,
My wife, won't let me!'

(*Speaking.*) All together now.

*Everyone sings along.*

There was I, waiting at the church,
Waiting at the church,
Waiting at the church;
When I found out he'd left me in the lurch,
Lor, how it did upset me!
All at once, he sent me round a note
Here's the very note,
This is what he wrote:
'Can't get away to marry you today,
My wife, won't let me!'

*Blackout.*


### SCENE TWO


*Eric is being interviewed.*

**Eric** It was a happy childhood. We were, are a happy
family. We all get on. Always have. Just a normal family.
Me dad went out to work, on the docks, and me mum
was at home. She had a few odd jobs now and again but
she was always there for us. Cooking, sewing, cleaning the
front step, looking after us. Or out in the neighbourhood
helping others. 'Go and take this round to Mrs So and
So's.' (*Beat.*) Is this really what you want . . . ? Oh okay.
I couldn't have asked for a better childhood. Me dad was
a bit of a dreamer. Used to tell us this story that he
stowed away on a ship to New York. We all knew it
wasn't true but we loved hearing it. (*Beat.*) We're just a
dead ordinary family. No big dark secrets. There'll be
much more interesting families round here you know.
(*Beat.*) So . . . er . . . I can't think of anything else.

## SCENE THREE

*8 Hope Place. Basement kitchen. Modern day. A bright spring day.*

*Maggie pins a picture on the kitchen cupboard in among photos, maps and the start of a very makeshift family tree with photos, drawings of faces and bits of string linking them together. There's a laptop open on the table surrounded by books and papers piled up. She's busy reading, checking things from laptop to books, scribbling down lists and drinking tea. She's still looking quite wild.*

*Simon comes in through the yard at the back. Maggie sees him at the back door window. He waves.*

**Maggie** Oh come in, come in. Hiya, love.

*Simon enters. He's got a bag with books and research with him.*

**Simon** Hiya. I've got some more info for you but it looks like you don't need it.

**Maggie** Been down the library and took out a few books meself. Even got a laptop now. Secondhand off Colin in the Chinese. I'm all hooked up to the internet. I've got a dingle and everything.

**Simon** D'you mean a dongle?

**Maggie** Yeah, whatever. It's amazing what you can find. All manner of crap. I keep on getting messages asking me if I want Viagra. What am I gonna do with that?

*Simon looks at the home-made family tree on the cupboards.*

**Simon** I love this.

**Maggie** I've started making a family tree of sorts on the cupboards. I've got me mother's side on this side and me dad's here. I've used any photos when I've got them and drawn a little picture if I haven't. A face with a hat and pipe is a man, rollers and lipstick a woman. I don't quite know what I'm doing, or what I'm looking for but . . .

*Simon sits down at the table and gets some papers out of his bag.*

**Simon**  I've found a few things for you.

**Maggie**  Great. Josie's gonna come round with hers so we can compare notes. She was a bit taken aback when I said I did want to know about our family now . . . Oh well.

**Simon**  Did you know there used to be a cemetery on this site? Before these houses were built.

**Maggie**  I do feel like it is haunted at the moment.

**Simon**  So, I found this. Bit surprising.

**Maggie**  Oh okay.

**Simon**  On a few censuses on your mother's side I noticed that there's these descriptions next to the names that have been blanked out. So I went back to the original records and the descriptions are still there. Here's some photocopies.

*He takes out some photocopied pages and lays them out on the table.*

**Maggie**  I love the way it's all handwritten out in fountain pen.

**Simon**  Here next to your grandmother's brother, James, James Kelly. See what it says? 'Imbecile.' He's only thirteen.

**Maggie**  Okay.

*She forces out a smile.*

**Simon**  Then here on the generation before, her mother's sister, Anne . . . Where is it? Here. Is down as 'feeble minded'.

*Maggie gets up and starts making tea. She's deep in thought.*

**Maggie** I'll . . .

**Simon** It's so wrong but . . . 'feeble minded'. I laughed at first. There was another one . . .

*He looks through his papers.*
  *Low rumbling. Maggie doesn't answer. She gets the tea things together in silence.*
  *Simon senses all is not well.*

You okay with this?

**Maggie** Yeah, fine. Well, no. I don't find it funny.

**Simon** Oh, I'm sorry.

**Maggie** It just means it's all true then, doesn't it. There's madness in the family. It's passed on down the line. It goes back to those idiots who thought Liverpool was New York and hasn't stopped.

**Simon** I don't think . . .

**Maggie** It proves it all. I am stupid.

**Simon** No, no. It's very much of the time, that's why they've crossed it out. It probably meant someone was dyslexic or . . .

**Maggie** You can't change history. You can try and cross it out but it's still there. I'm surprised it doesn't say it next to my name. 'Stupid', 'thick', 'waste of time'.

**Simon** Margaret.

**Maggie** What have I been good for? Cleaning and looking after people. That's all I'm good for.

**Simon** Maybe this isn't such a good idea? You're going to find out things you'd rather not know.

*Maggie drifts off in deep thought. Rumbling. Lottie comes alive in the corner of the kitchen. She's gripping the sink.*

**Lottie** Me nerves. Me nerves are bad today. Where are me . . . ? Get me me pills.

*Then she disappears. The rumbling subsides.*

**Simon** Do you want to stop this for now? We don't have to do any more.

**Maggie** No, I have to keep going. I have to.

*Maggie goes back to the books and laptop, determined. Blackout.*


### SCENE FOUR

**Veronica** One by one we moved away. Not very far, West Derby, Mossley Hill, Huyton. Well, apart from Frances who emigrated to the other side of the world. I don't know what we did wrong but she just wants nothing to do with us. She just upped and left one day without a word. How dare she? Makes me so angry. Maggie was the last one there. She nearly left this one time. This was when me dad was ill in the eighties. There was this bloke, who wanted her to go away with him but she always put the family first. I don't know if she regrets that now. She was great with me mother those last few years. Me mother was in quite a bad way towards the end and her memory was . . . Sometimes she'd be still sharp as a pin, other times she'd been talking to us like we were little kids. The people who've been through this house. (*Beat.*) But Maggie got to stay here and keep the house. I sometimes wish I'd never left.


### SCENE FIVE

*8 Hope Place. Basement kitchen. Modern day.
Maggie is buttering crumpets. Simon is at the table*

*pulling out more research he's done. They're both much more relaxed.*

**Maggie** We need crumpets now.

**Simon** Ah, ta. (*Playful.*) The service here is great. Do you want to hear what else I've found?

**Maggie** Am I going to regret it?

**Simon** I really don't know.

**Maggie** Give it to me.

*She brings the crumpets across to the table. They eat them with their cups of tea.*

**Simon** Here's a copy of your dad's birth certificate. He was born at – (*reading*) '144a Brownlow Hill'.

**Maggie** Just along the road.

**Simon** He didn't go far.

**Maggie** Whereabouts is 144a . . .?

**Simon** It's where the Catholic cathedral was built.

**Maggie** The irony, he couldn't stand the cathedral. Was there a house or a hospital there before?

**Simon** No, no. On that site was . . . the workhouse. It looks like he was born in the workhouse.

*Pause. Low rumble. A tortured crying Richard appears in the corner.*

**Richard** Elizabeth. My Elizabeth.

*He disappears. The rumble subsides.*

**Simon** Had you not heard that before?

**Maggie** He never said anything about his family. I thought he was brought up by an aunt . . . I don't even know if he had any brothers or sisters. It was never to be spoken about.

**Simon** I found this book. Here's a picture of it.

*Simon shows Maggie some pictures of it.*

**Maggie** It's huge.

**Simon** It went all the way along Mount Pleasant down Brownlow Hill. It was the largest workhouse in Europe. Four thousand people. And look. (*He finds the page.*) There's a brick wall that was part of the workhouse that's still there today. D'you think he knew he was born there?

**Maggie** He must have.

**Simon** Is that why he wouldn't go near the place? Hated it.

**Maggie** And what about his mother? Does it say anything about her?

**Simon** It looked like she died in there. TB.

*He passes Maggie another certificate. She looks at it.*

And he had two sisters who died there too.

*Maggie looks at the death certificates.*

**Maggie** (*reading*) 'Lucy, aged two years. Died of water on the brain. Ruth, aged six months. Died of diarrhoea.' To die of diarrhoea.

**Simon** If you were unmarried or had no family to go to, or were just really poor, that's where you ended up. There were no benefits then. (*He reads.*) 'Husbands and wives were split up, so they didn't "breed". Children were separated from their parents, to make them into useful human beings.' You lived in fear of ending up there. It was like a prison for being poor.

*Maggie thinks.*

I imagine there'd have been a lot of shame . . .

**Maggie** (*half to herself*) Maybe I've got more in common with him than I think.

*She tops up their tea from the pot.*

I don't know anything about your family. I bet you're the spoilt baby of the family, aren't you?

**Simon** There's only me really. I haven't really got a family.

**Maggie** There must be more than you. You an only kid?

**Simon** Yeah, yeah.

**Maggie** And what about your mum and dad? You must have come from somewhere.

**Simon** I was adopted . . . (*Pause.*) Shall we look at . . .?

**Maggie** You can ask all the questions but you don't like answering them, do you, eh?

**Simon** Maybe not. My adopted parents were . . . well, pretty uptight. Cold. My childhood was just so . . . quiet. They never really did anything with me, we never saw anyone else, there was no fun. I really don't know why they adopted me. They weren't horrible to me just . . . I am still in touch with them but there's no great desire for us to see each other, from me *and* them. (*Beat.*) I tried to trace my real, blood parents but . . . my mum had died. She was from over here, Liverpool. Drink and drugs from what I gather. And there's no father down on my birth certificate. And no one else.

**Maggie** You poor thing.

**Simon** I'm a historian with not much of a history, you could say.

**Maggie** You do come out with some clever stuff. It seems you're part of our family now, whether you like it or not.

**Simon** (*half throwaway*) I quite like it.

*Pause.*

**Maggie**  I would have loved to have had kids.

**Simon**  You'd have made a great mum.

*Pause. A moment between them. They hear the front door open and close as Josie enters from upstairs. They both listen out.*

**Josie**  (*off*) Auntie Margie? It's Josie.

**Maggie**  Down here.

*Josie heads down to the kitchen. Simon gets up.*

**Simon**  She shouldn't really see me here.

**Maggie**  Why ever not?

*Josie comes in.*

**Josie**  Hiya. (*She sees Simon.*) Simon, you're here?

**Simon**  Yeah, Margaret, Maggie, Margie, just asked me to help her with some history . . .

**Josie**  It's fine. I'm just surprised, that's all. It's fine. Hiya, Auntie Margie.

*She gives her a kiss.*

**Maggie**  Hiya, love.

**Josie**  Simon.

*She kisses him. It's very stiff and awkward.*

**Simon**  I've been meaning to call . . .

**Josie**  It's just funny. You said you're too busy to meet up but you're here with my auntie.

**Maggie**  Now that's my fault. I asked him to help me. I'm taking the blame for that.

**Josie**  But he could still return my calls.

**Simon** I'm sorry. I've just been . . .

**Josie** Busy, yeah.

*She looks at the family tree on the cupboards.*

So you wanted to know about the family tree? Seems like you've got it covered here.

*Blackout.*


## SCENE SIX

**Jack** It was a happy place to grow up. I just remember playing out in the streets all the time. Out the back in Rice Street, along Hope Street or down in the cemetery at the cathedral. We're talking from five, six, seven years old. Can you imagine that now? Me and Eric'd be down in amongst the gravestones pretending to be vampires and sometimes the cocky watch would come after us. We'd have to climb the quarry wall to get away from him. I can't believe we climbed all the way up. It must be about thirty feet. It was like a playground for us. Or sometimes we'd all go out, all us kids together. Our Peg would put the little ones in one of those Silver Cross prams and push us all the way down the hill and take us across on the ferry to New Brighton. Usually if it was all kicking off at home between me mum and dad. Peg and Veronica would be like, 'Let's get away from here.' (*Beat.*) But considering how much me mum and dad argued they still went on to have six kids. But then our Peg said that after their rows there was a lot of making up to be done. She was always looking after us, our Peg. It was like she was another mother sometimes. I don't know who was looking out for her.

*Caption:*

**HERE**

1962

*Temperance Hall – that was to become the Everyman Theatre. Lottie sitting at a bar. A barman, Roger, appears.*

**Roger** What can I get you, love?

**Lottie** What is there? I've never been to a place like this before. What have you got?

**Roger** Well. No booze.

**Lottie** (*playing along*) Really? In a Temperance Hall? That's a shame.

*He laughs.*

**Roger** We've got black beer and tonic, blood tonic, cream soda, ginger beer, sarsaparilla . . .

**Lottie** Oh go on. I'll try a sarsaparilla.

*He makes the drink.*

I don't even know what sarsaparilla is.

**Roger** Neither do I. I think it's from a root of some sort.

**Lottie** It's nice here.

**Roger** We haven't been here long but there seems to be a need here in this city.

**Lottie** You can say that again.

**Roger** It's somewhere different, isn't it? If you wanna go out and not drink.

**Lottie** I remember it when it was the picture house. Used to send the kids here on a Saturday morning.

*He hands her the drink. She takes a sip.*

Oh, it's nice that.

**Roger** There's a book over there people can sign. Make a pledge of temperance, if you want.

**Lottie** Oh, I'm not here for . . . It's not for me. I'm just waiting for me husband to arrive. He said he'd come. Got me sister babysitting and everything. (*She looks round. Pause.*) He's probably in the pub. (*Pause.*) He's not gonna come, is he?

*Blackout.*


### SCENE EIGHT

*Veronica interviewed by Simon. He is present this time.*

**Veronica** I miss the house and being surrounded by everyone. There's just me and Josie now and she's been away travelling seemingly for ever. My other daughters emigrated to the other side of the world, so I hardly ever see them or my grandkids. Ever since my Ron died it's never quite been the same. I feel like I'm on my own a lot . . . I love it when we get together. It's just like old times. Jack telling us his funny stories. Maggie looking after us. Eric getting all angry in the corner. I don't know where all that anger comes from. He was such a happy kid and then . . . Me mum found it hard to cope with having so many children, I think. It felt like a big family. Six kids but loads of families I knew had eight, ten, twelve. I knew a couple who had fifteen kids. Can you imagine?

**Simon** Sorry, you said six children, you mean five?

**Veronica** Yeah, yeah, there were four girls but now it's three.

**Simon** There was another daughter?

**Veronica**  Yeah. Little Elizabeth.

**Simon**  No one's ever mentioned her.

*The defences go up.*

**Veronica**  You can understand why. She died when she was only a baby. There was a fire in the house. We don't like talking about it.

**Simon**  I'd like to hear more about her if you don't mind.

**Veronica**  Actually I do mind. Shall we leave it there? D'you wanna turn it off?

**Simon**  I was just going to ask . . .

**Veronica**  I think I've said enough. Turn it off.

**Simon**  Right, of course.

*He stops the recorder.*


### SCENE NINE

*8 Hope Place. Basement kitchen. Modern day. Early evening.*

*The table is clear apart from a few books and laptop. The makeshift family tree is still on the cupboards. It has grown.*

*Veronica stands impatiently at the open back door smoking. A large, lidded pan sits simmering on the cooker. She drags on her cigarette and waits. Jack and Eric come in through the front door.*

**Jack**  (*off*) Hello. Peg?

**Veronica**  There's only me here. I'm down here.

*Jack and Eric come down the stairs into the kitchen.*

**Eric**  Is she not here?

**Veronica**  No sign of her.

**Eric**  What's this all about? Why have we all been summoned?

**Veronica**  Who knows. I can't wait around all day.

**Jack**  Have you got to be somewhere?

**Veronica**  Well, no, but . . .

**Eric**  What did she say to you?

**Jack**  Just got this text message, 'Can you make this date? I need to speak to you.'

**Veronica**  Same here.

**Jack**  I didn't even know she knew how to text.

**Veronica**  Getting us all here like this. All mysterious. Who does she think she is? Angela fuckin' Lansbury?

**Jack**  I reckon she's changed her mind about the house and she wants to apologise. That'll be it.

**Eric**  Believe that when I see it.

*Pause.*

**Jack**  Any word from . . .?

*Eric shakes his head.*

**Veronica**  Who? What you talking about?

**Jack**  (*to Eric*) Haven't you told her?

**Eric**  I don't wanna talk about it.

**Jack**  (*quiet to Veronica*) Pru's . . . left him.

**Veronica**  Oh. She hasn't. No one ever tells me anything. Am I always the last to be told? Why? What happened this time?

**Eric**  I don't wanna talk about it.

**Veronica**  Did you . . .

93

**Eric**  Veronica.

*Jack sees the family-tree creation on the cupboards.*

**Jack**  What the hell's this?

**Veronica**  God only knows.

*Jack looks at it closely.*

**Jack**  It's a family tree. Our family tree. There's me, you, and you, Peg. Mum's side here, me dad's side there. That's dead clever that.

**Veronica**  What's it for? Some kids' art project?

**Jack**  Ooh, what's that cooking?

*Jack lifts up the lid to the pan and looks inside.*

Scouse. Ah, smell that. Who's this for?

*The smell wafts through the theatre.*

**Veronica**  I don't know. Who knows what's going on here?

**Jack**  D'you think I can have a bit? No, I shouldn't. But no one will notice. Just a little mouthful, a taste. Look at it, there's loads. I'll stir it round so you can't tell. What d'you reckon?

**Eric**  Just friggin' taste it if you want to.

*Jack gets a spoon out of a drawer and takes a big mouthful.*

**Jack**  Hmm. Delicious. (*He takes another.*) Hmm. (*And another.*) Oh yeah.

**Veronica**  Are you going to eat it all?

**Jack**  No, no. I'm starving though. I've only had a pastie from Sayers all day. You see, she's made us scouse like old times. It's the old Peg back. It's gonna be fine.

**Eric**  You should write for Mills and Boon.

*They hear footsteps in the back.*

**Veronica** Oh ee ah.

*Jack takes one last mouthful.*

**Jack** Hmm.

*He gives the spoon a wipe and puts it back in the drawer.*

None the wiser.

*He moves about, not sure where to stand.*

What should we do?

**Eric** Nothing. It's only our friggin' sister.

*Jack stops still. Maggie comes in through the back door. She's got a brown-paper bag with some fresh bread inside. She looks bright and lively.*

**Maggie** Oh, you're all here. One of the advantages of you all having your own keys.

**Eric** Yes, we're here. As instructed. So what the fuck's this all about then?

**Maggie** Good to see you too, Eric. Have a seat. You don't need to stand on ceremony.

**Eric** I don't know how long we're staying. You're being very cryptic.

**Maggie** Am I? I don't mean to be.

**Veronica** I'm just going to . . .

*Veronica opens the back door and lights another fag.*

**Maggie** Popped out to get some crusty bread. I've made us a pan of scouse. And you can't have it without some crusty bread. There's a new posh bakers opened along the road. I went to get some 'artisan bread'.

**Jack** What the frig's that?

**Veronica** Three quid, full of seeds, nuts and bits of wood. One bite and your teeth are across the room. That's artisan bread.

**Maggie** It is lovely and they're all so passionate about it in there. These young kids who just love baking.

**Veronica** Passionate about baps?

**Maggie** Anyhow, you all up for some of this?

**Veronica** What is this? The last friggin' supper?

**Eric** I don't think we're staying long.

**Veronica** I'm not hungry.

**Maggie** Oh. Jack? You'll have some won't you? You love scouse, especially mine.

*Eric and Veronica look at Jack, pressurising him to say no.*

**Jack** I think I'm fine.

**Maggie** That's not like you. Why don't you have a taste? One mouthful and you'll want more.

*She stirs it and has a taste.*

It's good.

**Jack** (*under his breath*) Oh God.

**Eric** He's just eaten, haven't you.

**Jack** Er, yeah.

**Maggie** When has that ever stopped you?

**Veronica** And he's on a diet.

*Jack gives Veronica a look.*

**Maggie** Really?

**Jack** (*to Veronica*) Really? (*To Maggie.*) Really.

**Maggie** Well I'm gonna put it all out. If you want some, it's here.

> *She gets the scouse together through the next section.*
> *Slicing bread on a bread board, beetroot and red*
> *cabbage on the table. Knives, forks, salt and pepper.*

So how are you all?

**Eric** Fine.

**Veronica** Fine.

**Jack** Yeah, fine.

**Maggie** You know what fine stands for? Fucked up, insecure, neurotic and egocentric.

**Veronica** You what?

**Jack** Maggie!

**Maggie** I found it on the internet. It's spot on, isn't it.

**Veronica** You're on the internet?

**Eric** I don't need this. Come on, let's stop beating around the bush. Have you changed your mind about the house, cos that's all we want to know.

**Maggie** This is not about the house.

**Veronica** Well, that's all we're interested in.

**Maggie** (*sarcastic*) That's nice isn't it?

**Eric** What is it then?

**Maggie** I just wanted to see you. My sister and brothers.

**Veronica** Is that it?

> *Maggie is distracted.*

**Maggie** She's not still in the larder, is she?

**Jack** Who?

**Maggie** Lola.

*Maggie goes into the larder.*

**Eric** You what?

**Veronica** See. She's mad. She's gone proper mad. She's been imagining a cat. Our old cat.

**Jack** What should we do?

**Veronica** I don't think we can humour her much longer. She needs help, professional help. Maybe she needs to be sectioned. For her own good.

*Maggie comes out of the larder with a cat – a real live cat – in her arms.*

**Veronica** Oh my . . .

**Jack** There is a cat?

**Maggie** Of course there is. (*To cat.*) I've told you about going in there and attacking me packets of food. She's a little bugger.

*Maggie takes it off towards the hall and stairs.*
*Jack and Eric look towards Veronica.*

**Veronica** Well, there wasn't. She must have just got it.

**Jack** Who's the mad one now?

**Maggie** (*off, to cat*) Go on, eat some food.

*She comes back in minus cat.*

**Veronica** (*to Maggie*) Where did it come from?

**Maggie** Just wandered in. She strolls off again sometimes but always comes back. I don't know who she belongs to.

**Veronica** We're all still very angry you know.

**Maggie** Join the club.

**Veronica**  What have you got to be angry about?

**Maggie**  How long have you got?

**Veronica**  Eric's seeing if he can get it turned round.

**Eric**  I've spoken to the housing association, they said you can change your mind at any time.

**Jack**  Have you thought about reconsidering?

**Maggie**  No, no.

**Jack**  Because maybe you signed it away a bit on the hoof, under pressure . . .

*Maggie doesn't answer. She puts the knives and forks out on the table.*

**Veronica**  You won't even think about it?

**Maggie**  What are you more concerned about – the house or me?

**Veronica**  It's just a house. A building.

**Maggie**  Exactly.

**Veronica**  I didn't mean it like that.

**Maggie**  They've been showing me flats. They've got some nice ones out in Crosby near the beach. I think I'd like that.

**Veronica**  Why wouldn't you want this house? None of us have got it, you're lucky.

**Maggie**  How am I? You all got to go off and have lives. I didn't have kids so I have to stay here to look after me mother and father. You all just assumed I'd do it.

**Veronica**  You could have said if you didn't want to.

**Maggie**  Really? Could I? (*Beat.*) The main reason . . . What I did want to talk to you about was . . .

**Veronica**  Here we go.

**Maggie**  I've been doing a lot of thinking . . .

**Veronica**  Oh right.

**Maggie**  And I've been meeting up with Simon . . .

**Veronica**  Simon? What about?

**Jack**  Will you let her finish a fuckin' sentence?

*Veronica goes to say something else but stops herself.*

**Veronica**  Go on.

**Maggie**  I've been looking into our family tree.

**Eric**  I thought you didn't wanna know?

**Maggie**  Well, I didn't then.

**Eric**  But you do now?

**Maggie**  Yeah.

**Veronica**  I see.

**Maggie**  Aren't I allowed to change my mind?

**Veronica**  (*pointing to the family tree*) Is that what this is about? Who did this?

**Maggie**  Me.

**Jack**  (*under his breath*) I think it's great. Although you could've found a better picture of me. I've got the fattest, roundest head on here . . .

**Maggie**  I've found out some really interesting things. And I'd like to know more. From you. About our family. Know what happened.

**Eric**  When? Where?

**Maggie**  All of it.

**Veronica**  I don't know what you're talking about.

**Maggie** What do you remember? What were me mum and dad like?

**Veronica** Are you for real? You knew them.

**Maggie** There's lots I can't remember and some stuff I've held on to . . . Some things I've found out and . . .

**Veronica** What d'you wanna know? He was a bit of a drinker. She liked an argument. They probably shouldn't have been together but they're dead now. It's all in the past.

**Maggie** It's not all in the past for me. It's very much in the present. I carry it round with me every day. Keeping it . . . hidden only feeds it.

**Veronica** I don't know what you're talking about.

**Margaret** And I've buried things so deeply I don't know what's true or not.

**Veronica** What's she talking about?

*They hear the muffled sound of voices out in the back yard.*

**Eric** What's that?

*They all listen. It's Josie and Simon having a row. They can't figure out who it is at first.*

**Simon** (*off, muffled*) Oh, don't start all that again.

**Josie** (*off, muffled*) Every other thing I ask you to do, you don't wanna know, but we get invited round to me auntie's and you can't get here quick enough.

**Veronica** It sounds like Josie.

**Jack** And what's-his-face, Simon.

**Veronica** I didn't know she was coming.

**Simon** (*off, muffled*) I can go home if that's what you want.

**Josie** (*off, muffled*) Now you're being . . .

**Simon** (*off, muffled*) I just think that it's a bit rude . . .

**Veronica** Are they having a row? They're having a row. Listen . . .

**Simon** (*off, less muffled*) Well, we're here now. Are we going in or what?

**Josie** (*off, less muffled*) We might as well. And I don't want to be any later . . .

**Eric** I don't wanna hear.

**Veronica** Shush, I can't . . . They're coming in. They're coming in.

> *Josie opens the back door and enters with Simon. They turn on the smiles.*

**Josie** Hiya.

**Simon** Hi, everyone.

**Veronica** What a surprise!

> *Pause. There's an edgy silence. Josie picks up on the odd atmosphere.*

**Josie** Is everything okay?

> *Jack can't help but let out a big laugh.*

What are you laughing at?

**Jack** Ignore me. Just something familiar.

**Josie** (*placing a bag of booze on the side*) Some beer and wine there.

**Maggie** Ah, ta, love. Glad you could make it.

**Josie** You all know Simon, don't you?

**Jack** The posh one?

**Simon** (*with a smile*) Yes, that's me, the posh one.

**Maggie**  This is ready now.

**Eric**  We're not staying.

**Veronica**  Not hungry.

**Jack**  (*under his breath*) Not allowed.

**Josie**  Don't be daft. Come on, sit down and have some food.

*Josie and Simon sit down. Jack and Veronica look towards Eric, effectively waiting for his permission.*

**Eric**  Maybe just a bite and then we'll go. But I don't want it to look like I'm happy about it.

**Maggie**  You can eat it with a grimace on your face.

*Eric sits down.*

**Jack**  (*under his breath*) Thank fuck for that.

*Veronica and Jack sit down too.*

**Maggie**  That's more like it.

**Simon**  I can't remember the last time I had this.

**Jack**  You haven't had anything till you've had our Peg's scouse.

*Maggie dishes up scouse for everyone, working her way round the table.*

**Simon**  I just wanted to say. Thanks for all speaking to me. I showed my tutor some of the interviews and he thinks it's great. Thinks we might be able to get it published.

**Veronica**  In a book?

**Simon**  Only an academic book, but still.

**Maggie**  Isn't that great? Did you interview Josie?

**Josie**  No. He's not interested in me . . . for this.

**Simon** I could still do, it's not all finished. It was mainly people who'd lived here. But I'd love to get some of you talking about coming here as a kid.

**Josie** Maybe.

**Maggie** Tuck in, don't wait for me. And help yourself to red cabbage and beetroot.

**Jack** Smell that. I'm salivating all over the place

**Veronica** Remember when we used to have blind scouse with no meat in it when times were hard?

*Maggie dishes out beers and drinks for everyone.*

**Maggie** Oh yeah. How is it?

**Eric** Hmm.

**Veronica** Fine.

**Simon** Lovely.

**Josie** Perfect.

**Jack** Isn't this great? Us all together in the family home, all getting on, like we've never been away.

**Veronica** Trust Jack to get all sentimental.

**Jack** You know I'm a romantic at heart.

**Veronica** Is that why you've been married four times?

**Maggie** I can take you all through the family tree, if you're interested. I've found out things that have made me look at me mum and dad in a different way.

**Eric** Well, that's good.

**Josie** We've found something new. You're gonna love this. You know you said me grandad talked about New York? How back in the day his relations never made it there but he did?

**Jack** God, the stuff he came out with.

**Eric** I believed him at the time, it's only years later . . .

**Josie** It's all true. He went.

**Jack** Naah.

**Maggie** He didn't.

**Josie** He did. We've got proof.

**Eric** It was just a stupid story.

**Simon** We can show you.

*Simon takes out some photocopies and shows Jack and Maggie.*

**Josie** These are photocopies of passenger lists to New York. Simon found them.

**Simon** Took some searching but . . .

**Josie** This is a cargo liner and they even had passengers. Twenty-pound passengers they were. And they even list stowaways.

**Josie** (*looking through the list*) Ee ah, go down . . . And here he is, Richard Byrne.

**Jack** No? The little . . .

**Josie** He really went there. He stowed away on a ship to New York.

**Simon** Took twelve days to get there. Must have been found and then sent back six weeks later. (*On another sheet.*) There he is on the way back.

**Maggie** What an amazing thing to do.

**Veronica** When was this?

**Jack** Must have been before he met me mother.

**Veronica** God, if he hadn't been caught and got sent back. We wouldn't exist.

**Jack** Can you imagine just popping down the river, climbing on to a ship and ending up in America?

**Eric** Incredible.

**Jack** The call of the sea. They say even as a kid he was always running away from home. He'd be found trying to hitch rides at crossroads with a knotted hankie, Dick Whittington style.

**Eric** Let me see.

*Eric takes the papers and looks at them closely.*

**Jack** I loved it when me dad used to take us all down the river.

**Maggie** He never took us. Just the boys, you and Eric.

**Jack** You were always helping me mum.

**Maggie** Not out of choice.

**Jack** (*to Veronica*) And you'd be too busy with your skipping games out back with Frances. 'The big ship sails' and 'On a mountain stands a lady . . . '

*Veronica starts singing at the top of her voice.*

**Veronica** (*singing*)
On a mountain stands a lady, who she is I do not know,
All she wants is gold and silver, all she wants is a fine young man.
Lady, lady, touch the ground,
Lady, lady spin around,
Lady, lady, touch your shoe,
Lady, lady, go right through.

**Eric** What you playing at?

**Veronica** I just felt like singing. One of me old skipping songs. That was good, that.

**Jack** I loved it down by the river. Me dad'd tell us about all the sights you'd see. Men coming off the ships holding up parrots, monkeys, canaries. All these souvenirs from far-off lands.

**Veronica** That's where Mary McGinty's marmoset came from.

**Jack** You could go anywhere in the world from here. Out into the Atlantic, then on to America, Africa, India, China . . .

**Maggie** It makes me think really fondly of him. This little adventurer. (*Beat.*) You know, I've realised that I've been carrying so much anger around towards him . . . But maybe I understand him a little more now . . . And I can forgive him.

**Eric** Forgive him for what?

**Jack** Come on, Eric. We never knew what he was going to be like . . . Sometimes it was . . . I've never said this before . . . frightening.

**Eric** I don't remember it like that. (*Aware of Simon's presence.*) And is this the time . . .

**Jack** Well, I do. And if our Peg wants to make peace with that, then that's okay.

*Simon looks at the photocopy.*

**Simon** So 1949. When did he meet your mum and get married?

**Maggie** Forty-nine?

**Veronica** That can't be the right date. Our Maggie was born in 1949.

*She takes the paper and looks at the date. She reads.*

Seventh of the sixth, 1949. When's your birthday?

*Maggie can't speak.*

**Jack** The day before.

**Veronica** No.

*Maggie looks at the paper. Rumbling starts again.*

**Maggie** No. Look at the date he left. I was born one day and he left the country the next.

*Pause. Maggie is silent.*

**Josie** Must be a different year.

**Jack** Or a mistake. He wouldn't just leave you and me mum.

**Maggie** Well, he did.

**Josie** I'm so sorry.

**Veronica** It could mean anything.

**Jack** And then he came back and had us all. After leaving you and me mum.

**Veronica** And she took him back.

**Eric** I told you you should have kept it in the past, didn't I? But you wouldn't listen.

*The rumbling increases.*

**Jack** Maybe he just couldn't cope with being a father. Couldn't cope with me mum and her rowing. It wouldn't have been about you. It could have been any of us.

*Tears run down Maggie's face.*

Don't cry, Peg.

**Maggie** Our Frances had the right idea, get away from all this and start again. This was a stupid idea. Stupid.

**Josie** Don't say that. It wasn't.

*Pause. They all eat the scouse in silence. It's all incredibly awkward.*

**Jack** I'm not so hungry now.

**Josie** We should try and eat. (*To Maggie.*) You've gone to so much trouble.

**Veronica** Yes. Pass me the crusty bread please, Simon.

**Simon** Sure.

*Simon passes some bread across the table to Veronica. They eat in silence. Pause.*

**Josie** It is lovely this scouse, though.

**Simon** One thing I don't understand, and tell me if this is none of my business . . . I was surprised to find out there was another sister.

**Veronica** Yeah, that is none of your business.

**Simon** Okay, sorry. (*Pause.*) It's just that there's so many stories in this family about all manner of things but one of the biggest events you never discuss.

**Jack** It's understandable we don't talk about it.

**Maggie** Maybe we should. Need to.

*Pause.*

**Josie** (*to Veronica*) You know, Mum, we never talk about me dad.

**Veronica** This is certainly not the time for that now, Josie.

**Josie** When is the right time?

**Veronica** I don't know, but I know it's not now.

**Josie** Can I book in an appointment for us to talk about it?

**Veronica** I don't need your cheek . . .

**Josie** I'm serious. All I know is he died of a heart attack when I was six. There's a few photos, nothing more. Is that the rule in this family? 'We don't talk about that.'

**Veronica** That was my way of dealing with it.

**Josie** Anything difficult we don't go near. Why d'you think your daughters are living over the other side of the world? That I spend my whole time travelling?

**Veronica** Oh, is it my fault, is it? I didn't know all the problems of the world all led back to me.

**Josie** You don't have to be so hard.

**Veronica** Yeah, Maggie, for once you're right. This was a stupid idea.

*She pushes her plate away and gets up to light a cigarette at the sink.*

And I'm gonna smoke it in here too. It's fuckin' freezing out there.

*Pause.*

**Josie** (*to Maggie*) I'd like to hear about your sister, you know.

**Veronica** Oh you're on one tonight, aren't you.

**Eric** Maybe we should take a leaf out of the Mancunians' book and learn that sometimes it's good to keep quiet, eh?

**Simon** I don't know if that's really what I was saying . . .

**Eric** Sometimes when I go into a shop for a paper I don't always want the whole life story of the girl behind the till, I just want the paper and go. But here everything turns into a whole friggin' pantomime.

**Simon** What's interesting is . . .

**Eric** (*to Simon*) I don't care what you find interesting, son. I don't know why you had to come here and do this. Interfering in our family. Churning all this up.

**Maggie** Eric. Why are you having a go at Simon?

**Eric** We were *fine* until he came along. With his history this and history that.

**Simon** I'm sorry if you think . . .

**Maggie** Fine. Fucked-up, insecure, neurotic and egocentric.

**Veronica** Will you stop saying that?

**Maggie** Clearly we weren't 'fine'. Harking back to some golden age of our family. Where everything was perfect.

**Eric** (*to Simon*) Why are you doing this? Is this what you wanted? For it all to kick off? You're loving this, aren't you. You're probably recording it too.

**Simon** No, I . . .

**Eric** What is it all about? You're not interested in her. (*Pointing at Josie.*) You just wanted this, didn't you? You're probably more interested in boys than girls.

**Jack** Eh, Eric, you've gone too far now.

**Maggie** I'm sorry, Simon, but I don't know what's got into me brother.

**Eric** Well . . .

**Simon** It's f— (*He goes to say 'fine' and corrects himself.*) Okay. You're an amazing family, that's all I know. And Josie, I don't want you to think . . .

**Josie** Not now, Simon, let's . . .

*Pause.*

**Simon** I think I should leave you all be . . .

**Maggie** There's no need for that.

**Simon** No, I feel I'm . . . This is family stuff. I'm not part of this family.

**Josie** Now you're being . . .

**Simon** No, no. I should. I'll catch you . . . See you all.

*He heads out and touches Maggie's arm on the way.*

See you, Margaret.

*Maggie gives him a little wave. He disappears out of the kitchen door. Pause.*

**Josie** I really didn't know there was another sister. Me mum had never mentioned her. What was her name? Elizabeth?

**Veronica** I must have.

**Josie** Never did.

**Maggie** She was lovely. Really gentle and quiet. This shock of blonde hair and bright blue eyes.

**Jack** You'd go over to her cot thinking she was asleep cos you hadn't heard a peep out of her for ages and she'd just be lying there. Eyes wide open, big smile on her face, happy as Larry.

**Josie** How old was she when . . .

**Eric** I don't think I need to hang around to hear this either.

*Eric gets up to leave.*

**Jack** Don't go, Eric.

*He stops and stands at the back. His back to them but still listening.*

**Maggie** She wasn't even one.

**Veronica** Seven months.

**Josie**  So, what . . . ?

**Maggie**  There was a fire. They managed to get to her and put it out before it really took hold but . . . the smoke had done it's damage. (*Pause.*) And it was all my fault.

**Jack**  You mustn't say that, Peg.

**Maggie**  Well, it was, I was meant to be looking after you all.

**Josie**  Where was your mum and dad?

**Maggie**  Me mum had gone to the shops for our tea. Or was out in the neighbourhood somewhere. Doing some good deed.

**Veronica**  She was always helping neighbours out. Sometimes it was like she had more time for them than she did for us.

**Maggie**  D'you think?

**Veronica**  She was far too concerned with what everyone else thought of her.

**Eric**  I thought she was in bed. Having one of her bad days.

**Veronica**  Was she?

**Maggie**  Me dad was at work.

**Veronica**  He was in the pub.

**Eric**  He was at work.

**Veronica**  He was in the pub.

**Josie**  And you were, how old?

**Maggie**  Eight. I was eight.

**Josie**  And you were meant to be looking after all the other kids?

**Maggie**  Well, yeah.

**Josie**  That's mad.

**Jack**  She did a good job.

**Maggie**  And all we know is that I forgot to put the fireguard in front of the fire. A spark must have leapt out and it all went up. I'd always put it there every other time. Don't know what happened. It was my job to do the fire. Cleaning out the grate. Cinderella here. No wonder I love me central heating now.

**Jack**  But it was warm. Spring. I remember me dad saying he didn't know why you'd even lit it in the first place.

**Maggie**  I can't remember much else. We weren't allowed to go to the funeral. Me mum and dad fought even more after that.

**Veronica**  It got really bad. They both blamed each other.

**Maggie**  No, they blamed me. He didn't really speak to me much again after that. Even right up until he died and I friggin' nursed him, he never had any time for me. (*It's coming back to her.*) Now I remember . . . I remember me mum finding out about the fireguard and going mad at me. Just there in the hall. Calling me stupid, stupid, stupid. I didn't even know why I felt so ashamed but that's it. Any shame I had, that day cemented it in me.

**Josie**  From her saying that one thing?

**Maggie**  It was my fault. That I was thick and that's why I did it.

**Josie**  You were eight years old!

*It's all too much for Maggie.*

**Eric**  You shouldn't blame yourself.

**Maggie**  I can't help it.

**Jack**  It's in the past.

**Maggie** How do you ever get over that? Elizabeth could still be here if it wasn't for . . .

**Eric** I lit it! I lit it! I lit the fire.

**Jack** You what?

**Veronica** No?

**Eric** It was me. Not you, me.

**Maggie** It can't have been. I remember doing it.

**Eric** I don't know how because it really was me. (*Pause.*) I always wanted to light the fire but it was always me dad or you. They'd never let me do anything. So I had a go meself. There was no one about and it was a warm day so it hadn't been lit. I did that thing me dad would do where he'd get a big double sheet of newspaper and put it across the fireplace to suck up all the air and really get it going. And it would just stay there, held up by the suction. Or the fire pixie as he called it. I was worried the newspaper would catch alight, I'd seen that happen with you or me dad. And it did, and I remember me little heart going, but I managed to get the paper off and into the fire before it did any damage. I was so proud of meself, I was made up. I wanted to show me dad what I'd done, wanted to see how happy he'd be, so I went to look for him. I was so relieved at the newspaper not burning the house down that I didn't think about the fireguard . . . The next thing I know is I'm outside in the yard with you and the house is . . . I'm so sorry.

**Maggie** Maybe I was told so many times that I really thought it was me. Why didn't you say? Why did you let me take the blame?

**Eric** I thought they blamed each other. I didn't know what to do.

**Maggie** From that moment, that was it . . . I've been a nervous wreck ever since.

**Eric** You shouldn't be. It was all my fault.

**Josie** It was nobody's fault. You were kids. It was an accident. If anyone's to blame it's your parents.

**Eric** Eh now . . .

**Maggie** Eric, you don't have to keep defending them.

**Eric** I know, I know.

*He starts crying. Maggie gets up and holds him. He cries into her arms.*

I'm so sorry, Maggie. I'm so . . .

*He continues to cry.*

**Maggie** Shush now. Shush.

*The others disappear until Maggie is left alone at the table.*
*We hear Young Maggie crying. Maggie looks for her and then spots her under the table at the front, hiding.*
*Maggie goes round to the front of the table and sees her young self. Young Maggie looks up to her.*

Don't cry. It's not your fault. It really isn't. You're just a kid. It's going to be okay. It will get better. I promise.

*Young Maggie wipes her eyes and stops crying and breathes.*

*Blackout.*